Celebritize Yourself:

The 3-Step Method to Increase Your Visibility and Explode Your Business

Marsha Friedman

Founder of the Marsha Friedman Celebritize Yourself Method™

Acclaim for Marsha Friedman's

Celebritize Yourself: The Three Step Method to Increase Your Visibility and Explode Your Business

"We live in a celebrity world. To take full advantage of what that world has to offer, read Marsha Friedman's astute analysis of how to turn yourself into a celebrity. It's a sure-fire formula for success."

—AL RIES, co-author, *War in the Boardroom*

"Personal Branding is one of the hottest ideas out there. But most so-called experts don't tell you enough. In her must read book, Marsha Friedman shows you how to transform your personal brand to celebrity status and how to reap the resulting rewards. Fame and fortune anyone?"

—DAVID MEERMAN SCOTT, bestselling author of *The New Rules of Marketing & PR* and the hit new book *World Wide Rave*

"*Celebritze Yourself* should be required reading for any professional who wants to stand out in a crowded marketplace. The truth is; celebrity isn't only for celebrities anymore. We have celebrity political pundits, celebrity cooks, lawyers, financial experts, fitness gurus, even celebrity bail bondsmen! *Celebritze Yourself* is a must read for any professional who wants to take full advantage of this new media age - and the New Age of Celebrity we live in!"

—LEE HABEEB, Co-Creator of *The Laura Ingraham Show* and Strategic Content Director of Salem Radio Network, which syndicates talk radio stars Michael Medved, Dennis Prager, Bill Bennett, Mike Gallagher and Hugh Hewitt

"In the current financial market Marsha Friedman's *Celebritize Yourself* is a perfectly timed new bible for any Executive or Entrepreneur looking to grow their business. A rush to read!"

—BERNY DOHRMANN, author of *Super Achiever Mind Sets & Perfection CAN Be Had*

"We live in an amazing new age of multidimensional communications offering the outgoing speaker unlimited opportunities to promote themselves, their businesses and their products. Marsha Friedman is a recognized master of modern media marketing who holds the key to these principles. Her marvelous book provides a concise and accurate roadmap for ambitious entrepreneurs to arrive at levels of fame and fortune previously only accessible to a relatively lucky few."

—MICHAEL HARRISON, Editor and Publisher, *Talkers Magazine*

"Marsha knows more about how to 'Celebritize' a writer or expert than anyone I have met. Now she has agreed to provide an easy to follow program that has a guaranteed result factor for the reader who follows her advice. More than worth the price and the effort!"

—SUZANNE CAPLAN,
Business Turnaround Consultant & Author

"Marsha's book, *Celebritize Yourself* gave me back my marketing mojo. It reminded me of principles and techniques I had forgotten that once turned The Ruff Times into the biggest-selling financial newsletter out there. Marsha's techniques really work and are worth millions!"

—HOWARD RUFF, New York Times best-selling author of
How To Prosper During The Coming Bad Years in the 21ˢᵗ Century
and founder of *The Ruff Times*.

"In today's Internet era, even though there are more media opportunities than ever before, it has become more challenging to get the attention. Anyone who wants to succeed by achieving prominent awareness must have a smart and practical plan. Marsha Friedman's *Celebritize Yourself* is your very own personal step-by-step strategic guide to capture the celebrity status you desire and deserve... starting with, 'it's okay for me to promote myself because I am special!' "

—DAVID HENDERSON, Communications Strategist and author of
The Media Savvy Leader

"Marsha Friedman's book is beautifully simple and she speaks from experience on every page. She has created a three step formula that will catapult you to success: Come up with a brilliant idea that people can really use, write a 'how to' book, and create lots of buzz through media appearances. I've used her system, and it works!"

—MARK SKOUSEN, Best Selling Author and Editor,
Forecasts & Strategies

"Marsha's method for building your visibility and exploding your business is a proven formula for success. Over the years, her company, EMSI, has applied these principles to me and my business and have made me a firm believer in her *Celebritize Yourself* method."

—ARNOLD S. GOLDSTEIN, PH.D. Bestselling author of
Asset Protection Secrets

"*Celebritize Yourself* is a must read book for anyone who wants to get ahead of the pack in their profession, industry or career."

—DR. EARL MINDELL, Best Selling Author of *Vitamin Bible*,
Herb Bible and *Prescription Alternatives*

"*Celebritize Yourself* is a fantastically inspiring MUST READ for anyone who has ever wanted to truly raise their profile as a leading expert in their industry or niche. The very best thing about the book is Friedman's willingness to share her remarkable and highly-lauded experience with others."

—NETTIE HARTSOCK, *Must Read Business Books*, Senior Editor
Allbusiness.com

"The notion of publicity and being a celebrity in your industry is a mystery to the average CEO. Marsha demystifies this concept, while clearly showing the value of achieving it, and providing strategies necessary to make it happen. Her advice is intended to get you through the long haul ---not just the first '15 minutes.' This will be required reading for all my clients and is a must read for any entrepreneur."

—MARIA SIMONE, Leading Business Strategist for Entrepreneurs
and CEO of "*Passion To Prosperity*"

"WARNING : USE OF THIS BOOK MAY LEAD TO FAME AND FORTUNE! It's in you. Hard earned knowledge and experiences that you – and only you – were put on this earth to share with others. You want to speak up, point out, fire up, and use what you know to help others and do so in a way that positively affects the most people possible. But how? Here's how... read Marsha Friedman's book *Celebritize Yourself: The Three Step Method to Increase Your Visibility and Explode Your Business.*

"This is not a stodgy, pie-in-the-sky, hard to read business book. Marsha has done something wonderful. Unique. She's delivered a business book elegant in its simplicity, that's full of real-life inspirational examples, yet ... easy to read and understand. But more importantly, that anyone – in any business – can use as a roadmap to share one's life experience with others who may be seeking the wisdom you have gained."

—STEVE KAYSER - Editor of the award-winning
Expert Access E-zine

"Marsha Friedman's *Celebritize Yourself* has taken the mystery and confusion out of the PR game! What a brilliant read!"

—JOY GENDUSA, author and CEO, *Postcardmania*

"*Celebritize Yourself* is an important read for anyone who wants to take their career to the next level. This method contains the ultimate blueprint for business and personal expansion!"

—JILL LUBLIN, international speaker and author of national
bestselling books, *Guerrilla Publicity, Networking Magic* and
Get Noticed... Get Referrals (McGraw Hill)

"*Celebritize Yourself* is a must read for anyone who wants to brand themselves and who understands the value of having their own book as a vehicle to do so!"

—ELLEN REID, Founder of *Ellen Reid's Book Shepherding*

Dedication:

This book is dedicated to Steve, my devoted husband who always believes in me, sometimes more than I believe in myself; my loving mom who showed me what a mother's love truly is; and in memory of my wonderful dad, who loved me unconditionally.

Table of Contents

Acknowledgements

Celebritize Yourself is the culmination of nearly twenty years of hands-on experience in helping people move closer to their business and personal goals. It's customary to acknowledge the people who contributed to a book, but it would be impossible to name all of the clients, friends, and business associates who played a role in the process.

I've learned so much from so many. Yet, one of the most important things I learned is that helping people gives me immense pleasure. So, having a PR firm that enables me to play a support role in so many lives has truly been an enormous gift.

Thanks to my husband, Steve, who joined the firm five years ago and has been an instrumental force since day one. Some people warned us of the possible decline of our marriage if we joined as partners in business... but they were so wrong! It's added a great new dimension to our marriage and has brought us even closer together! Steve, I love you and thanks for being my partner on this journey!

To my wonderful sons, Damon and Elon, who have generously supported my entrepreneurial spirit. You're the light of my life and I cherish you both dearly. I feel so fortunate to be your mom! To my daughter-in-law, Rachel, thank you for bringing my beautiful grandson into the world - you're a blessing to our family in more ways than I can count. I'm forever grateful!

And, thanks to my wonderful staff who play a key role in my life and the life of our clients – most especially, Rich Ghazarian, Ginny Grimsley, Lisa Hess, Chris Tompkins, Damon and Rachel Friedman and Cheryl Smith. Your dedication, caring and professionalism has made this business a joy to operate.

Thanks to Rusty Fischer who helped me put this project together – your patience and understanding made it so easy to work together.

To my dear friend, Arnold Goldstein, for your wonderful editorial help; your friendship and support of this project was an enormous contribution.

And, lastly, very special thanks to the brilliant humanitarian and philosopher, L. Ron Hubbard, who through his works taught me about caring and responsibility, courage and integrity – all of which gave me the knowledge to grow as a person and build a successful business. His great teachings have played one of the most vital roles in my life.

I've been motivated and inspired by all who have touched my life on this journey – and if this book succeeds to motivate and inspire others it will be my greatest reward.

Who is This Book For?

Celebritizing Yourself is about branding yourself as an expert. Yes, to become a celebrity is no easy feat, but in today's world, it is easier than ever. Thanks to the popularity of talk show formats on radio and major network TV, the highly specialized programming on cable TV, the explosion of Internet shows, Web site online PR and marketing, the countless newsletters and industry conventions and about a bazillion speaking groups all seeking a strong, interesting topic for their next seminar, keynote or sponsorship, there are more ways to become a celebrity than there are, well, celebrities!

Anyone – in any business – can become a celebrity following my proven 3-Step Method. Anyone from the homeless to the candy shop clerk to the housewife to the professor to the entrepreneur to the CEO can become a celebrity – they already have! To celebritize oneself is not merely to gain fame or fortune. It's to share one's life experiences with others who may be in search of, and in need of, your wisdom. That's the guiding philosophy for becoming a celebrity. The satisfaction is its own reward.

Introduction:

Everyone Has a Celebrity Within Them!

Y ou've heard their names:

- Zig Ziglar. Salesman-turned-author-turned-celebrity.
- Suze Orman. Stockbroker-turned-author-turned-celebrity.
- Bob Greene. Fitness expert-turned-author-turned celebrity.

The list of ordinary folks who became extraordinary celebrities is endless. Here's the big question: What do these celebrities from very different backgrounds have in common? (Besides their whopping incomes, that is!) Zig Ziglar, Suze Orman, Bob Greene, and hundreds of other household names all share the innate power to "celebritize" themselves. They are masters at turning their specialized, valuable knowledge into profits and their expertise into fame and fortune.

Here's a more important question: What do these three experts-turned-authors-turned-celebrities have in common with *you?* Well, like you, they started out as experts in their respective fields before they ever sold one book. Perhaps like you, they had a burning passion to spread the word, share their life experiences, and change people's viewpoints about what they had to say, and they did it in a way that positively affected the **greatest number of people possible.**

So, what do *you* know that can help others? Is it something about business? Health? Finance? Law? Cooking? Cleaning? Candlestick making? Celebrity authors spring up from every walk of life, every sex, race, color and creed, and every type of business or occupation imaginable. Never for a moment think that you don't possess unique and valuable knowledge that can greatly benefit others. You have that powerful message within you!

Let me tell you about my own awakening moment. I talk to many people every day to advise and counsel them about how they can better promote themselves, or their books, company, and products. Yet it wasn't until I addressed a large audience one day and had people approach me afterward to express their appreciation for my talk and how much they learned – that I realized how valuable the information is that I have at my fingertips and how important it could be to so many others.

I realized, also, that each and every one of us knows something that would be valuable to others. And, most assuredly, there are thousands – or maybe even millions – of people waiting to get this vital information from you!

Dale Carnegie first spoke publicly while working as a struggling actor. Rachel Ray sold candy at Macy's before becoming one of America's bestselling cookbook authors and TV personality. Linda Cobb ran a home restoration business before she penned the bestselling *Talking Dirty with the Clean of Queen.* Her empire now includes half a dozen sequels.

You don't even have to be employed to celebritize yourself. A tiny

Ohio newspaper offered Erma Bombeck a paltry $3 a column; she became America's most celebrated housewife who later authored over a dozen bestsellers. Kaile Warren, founder of Rent-A-Husband, was homeless before celebritizing himself and becoming an Oprah favorite!

I could go on and on. As CEO of a national publicity firm, Event Management Services, Inc. (EMSI), I happily share my knowledge distilled from years of experience in helping people and companies celebritize themselves. Many of my clients start as experts, wind up as authors, and enjoy the entire transformation of being celebritized. You can too through my new book, *Celebritize Yourself: The 3-Step Method To Increase Your Visibility and Explode Your Business.*

The 3-Step Method at the heart of *Celebritize Yourself* is based on my years of personal research and a lifetime of expertise that comes from guiding individuals much like you. And what are these 3 Steps?

- Step 1: *Write!*
- Step 2: *Speak!*
- Step 3: *Sell!*

Zig, Suze and Bob – not to mention Rachel, Erma, Kaile and Linda – shared the innate ability to celebritize themselves. But all seven became authors first, celebrities second. Thus, **Step # 1** of my process is to *write, write,* and *write* more. (Or have someone write for you!).

Did you ever hear the expression, "When a tree falls in the woods, does anybody hear it?" Books are written to be read. Today's successful authors-turned-celebrities know that to bridge the gap between published author to celebrity status requires one to be heard also. Thus, **Step 2:** *Speak.* That means as often as possible and as many audiences as possible; on stages, in the media and on the Web.

Finally, **Step 3** includes the essence of celebrity. In one form or another you must **Sell.** Authors sell books, movie stars sell tickets, singers sell CDs, sports figures sell sports drinks, CEOs sell their products, professionals sell their services, but every celebrity sells, sells, and sells some more! So will you! You will sell your books, products, services or whatever... and each time you sell, you also sell *yourself.*

Marsha Friedman
marsha@celebritizeyourself.com
www.celebritizeyourself.com

Chapter 1:

Isn't it Time You Walked into the Limelight?

"Get started now. With each step you take you will grow stronger and stronger, more and more skilled, more and more self-confident, and more and more successful... But you have to take action to get it."

~ Jack Canfield & Mark Victor Hansen, *The Aladdin Factor*

This thing we call "celebrity" need not be momentary – particularly not as brief as Andy Warhol's acclaimed 15 minutes! Done smartly, celebrity (fame) can last a lifetime. There is no shelf life for the true celebrity. Mike Wallace, Chick Corea and John Grisham are absolute pros who, like the Energizer bunny, bounce back year after year with great new stuff, be it hard-hitting news, top jazz CDs, or best-selling legal thrillers.

You may not read about these celebrities in the gossip rags each week, but they're always there, nonetheless, just under the public's radar, quietly doing their job with integrity, calm, and perseverance that earns them credibility and respect wherever they go. To simply know their name is to know them – what they stand for, who they are, and what they do. Longevity, or "staying power," is an important quality for the true "celebrity."

Although "Celebrity" can oftentimes have negative connotations, when I use the word "celebrity" throughout this book, think about someone entirely different than the mega stars, tabloid seekers or the 15-minute celebrity.

Our celebrity is someone who is trying to gain recognition for all the right reasons, and is eager to help others improve their lives. Specifically, I want you to start thinking about someone like... yourself. You are someone with expert knowledge, a desire to share, and the willingness and ability to express yourself to a vast public that needs whatever information you have to offer.

Yes there are monetary rewards to be had and why shouldn't you receive something valuable in exchange for your effort to help others? There's nothing wrong with that.

Nor is it shameful to want celebrity status. Why blush, stammer or make excuses? If you're not a celebrity in your field, someone else will be. So, why not fess up and start becoming a celebrity today? That's the first step: you must <u>want</u> to be one! So, let's superimpose your face to your name and your name to the word: celebrity. There, the vision is taking hold.

Empowering isn't it?

Good. Because to *become* a celebrity, you must first truly *decide* to be a celebrity. And that may mean making some changes, beginning with your attitude about yourself. For celebrity status to work – and it will work – enthusiastically achieve this first goal so you can successfully complete this journey.

"But, if it's so easy, why doesn't everybody become a celebrity?!?" you might ask.

Great question, and within the answer lies the secret. Most people view celebrities, pop stars, authors, TV commentators, talk show hosts, famous doctors and lawyers, and so forth, and think, "I could do that." And between you, me, and the fence post, they're probably right.

Case in point: I love dancing. I particularly love watching movies (or TV shows) with lots of dancing. So, when the Antonio Banderas movie, *Take the Lead,* was released, I was among the first to show up on opening night. In one poignant scene midway through the movie, one of Antonio's inner city dance students complained, "Good stuff like that only happens to other people."

Antonio's response: "You're right; good stuff happens to the people who show up to get it."

There, in a nutshell, is the big secret. As simple as it sounds, that's the secret to celebritizing yourself. The difference between you and every celebrity you watch, read, hear, or see is not that they're prettier, smarter, richer, taller, shorter, thinner, have better connections, or are more photogenic. The one important difference is that they acted upon their dreams. They showed up. They got what they wanted.

Yes, other factors may have played a role in crafting their celebrity. Talent, hard work, perseverance, luck, networking, connections, savvy, street smarts, research, etc., are all factors. But boil it down, cool it off, shake it loose, and examine what remains. Check the origin to each success story and you will see that deciding to play the game and to "show up" to play it is ground zero of day one for Celebrity 101.

So if you're truly ready to start, then congratulations; you're on your way. You've already mastered the art of showing up.

You're here! You're reading! You're learning!

But showing up is only the starting point. It's as important to stay there; and that, my friends, is the hard part. No one better illustrates this than an early client who has remained a friend. I first met Ben after he co-wrote his first book, had his own local radio show, and was well known for his expertise, both locally and nationally. Shortly thereafter, his co-author sued him, which threatened everything he was building. The foundation of his career was crumbling – or so I thought!

Ben fought fiercely to keep his dream alive, despite his own personal demons. Today Ben's looking to host a national TV show on a major network! Had Ben gone down for the count as most people might have done, the celebrity-dom he sought would perhaps have been lost forever.

When I share Ben's story, I invariably get one of three reactions: some nod with understanding and think, "I could have done that," others think, "I *already* do that," and still others blanche, "No way could I have ever done that."

But, my friend Ben wasn't going to let anyone destroy his vision. He decided to be the expert, go the full route and become a celebrity in his field. No one would take away his dream. Ben, always true to his vision, will now reap the harvest.

What enabled him to stay in the ring? His self-identity as a celebrity. He never let go. My point: to celebritize yourself you must stubbornly think of yourself as one. It all starts with you. How you perceive yourself creates the reality. See yourself as a celebrity and so too will others!

With this book you will make yourself a well-known and well-positioned expert in your field. The process is what I call "celebritizing yourself." "Celebritizing" is more than a mere buzz word or phrase. It is a practical system to make your career dreams come true.

Soon you'll see how. But for now, try a small experiment: with the next person you see (not just the next familiar, open, friendly face you see; say, in your living room or at the office, but the very next face) – smile and say, "I'm writing a book!"

It might be your child's school teacher, your doctor, lawyer, neighbor, mailman or even a complete stranger; but until you take great pride in what you're trying to do – until you can smile, introduce yourself and proudly say, "I'm writing a book!" – achieving celebrity status will just never be a comfortable process to you. To be a celebrity in your field means to transform yourself into the center of attention. It's about speaking up, pointing out, listening in, responding positively and always, **always** using your special knowledge to help others. In the process, you will not only have to do a lot of talking, but you will have to do a lot of talking about yourself. Sorry; that's just part and parcel of celebritizing yourself.

I'm reminded of another dear friend, now deceased, who wouldn't mind me talking about him if he knew it could help you. His name was Harry Browne. Harry was not a household name to most people, but in the world of personal finance, he was a star. Harry wrote several best-sellers in the '70s and '80s and remained a favorite speaker well into the '90s. He also made his mark in politics and in 2001 took on the thankless task of running for President of the United States on the Libertarian ticket.

I first met Harry in the late '70s at a financial conference that I had helped organize. I always knew that Harry was a brilliant man when it came to finance, the economy, politics, and even philosophy. But once I got to know him better I realized what I admired most about Harry was how he truly cared for people and his devotion to help people lead richer, happier lives.

I watched Harry speak to huge audiences and, afterward, have throngs of people throw questions at him while he descended the stage. As I stood aside him on many occasions, I was always impressed with how willing he was to share himself, to answer questions, and to provide whatever knowledge he could. He knew how important his role was to these people, and he never let them down. Harry's success "secret," I believe, was that he genuinely cared and demonstrated a strong, innate purpose to help people improve their lives. He would have made a great president!

Now, Harry understood the importance of being a celebrity for all the right reasons – particularly in a world where people often become celebrities for the wrong reasons. The celebrity you want to be is the one who wants to share knowledge and help people to live a better life. We only talk about ourselves because we are the messengers. Whether our business ignites us, our cause excites us or our organization, charity or foundation delights us, we seek to celebritize ourselves so that as many people as possible hear and benefit from our message.

But is there ever a message without a messenger?

And how will people ever hear it if we don't speak up?

When you try my experiment, you'll be quite surprised that so many people will be genuinely interested in what you have to say and, particularly, what you are writing about. I suggest you try this experiment before you take Step 1 of the *Celebritize Yourself* process because I know the response will be so overwhelmingly positive.

Try it; see for yourself! Note the looks on people's faces when you tell them you're writing a book. You'll then be inspired to tell more and more people and with that momentum you're already well on your way to celebritizing yourself!

The key to this experiment is practice and lots of it. And remember, when you talk about yourself you're really NOT talking about yourself. You're talking about the new and exciting book you're writing; a book with a message that's uniquely yours is what will make you a unique celebrity.

So, much like the way I tried to change your viewpoint about "celebrity" in this chapter, I also want to change how you feel about talking about yourself. Remember, you're really not talking about yourself; you're simply opening a dialogue about what you know, what you learned, what you have to offer and how you can help your listener. When people understand the importance of their message and truly believe it, they are encouraged to shout from the nearest rooftop: "I'm writing a book!"

You say you aren't ready for this yet? Then try this pre-experiment: Don't tell the next person you meet. Instead go to a mirror, smile, and say, "I'm writing a book!"

Still feels pretty good, huh? You. Writing. A Book!!! (Gulp!) Hard to believe? Well, it's easier than you think. But you probably won't write a book without some help. That's where I come in. So if you're ready – and there's no time like the present – let's together take the first steps to celebritize yourself...

Celebritize Yourself Fact:

"Whether our business ignites us, our cause excites us or our organization, charity or foundation delights us, we seek to celebritize ourselves so that as many people as possible hear and benefit from our message."

Chapter 2:

The Joy of Becoming the Celebrity in Your Field

ce·leb·ri·ty *(n) a famous or celebrated person*

We can attempt to define the term 'celebrity' until the sun goes down, but what does it mean – really – to be a celebrity? Do you envision red carpets or velvet ropes? VIP access or paparazzi? Sunglasses or limousines? Supermarket tabloids or CNN scandals?

'Celebrity' means different things to different people. But what DOES it really mean to be a celebrity in your field?

Often we see the gulf between what we do and what mega-star celebrities do as so wide we could never bridge that gulf to reach that fabled world of celebrity-dom. But by discussing 'celebrity' – by defining its terms – and identifying the different types and levels of celebrity one can achieve, then we make it tangible to ourselves and to others and we also make it attainable.

So in this chapter, let's discuss what it means to be a celebrity in your own field – whether you're a doctor, financial advisor, real estate broker, used car salesperson, or even a waiter. You can celebritize yourself – as you will soon see – <u>in any field.</u>

Likewise, anyone can rise to the top of their field and become the well-known "expert" – THE "go-to" person in that industry. That recognition – becoming well-known and respected for your knowledge – is what "celebrity" is all about.

Celebritize Yourself Fact:
"'Celebrity' means different things to different people."

Celebrity: It's Not Just for Movie Stars Anymore!

It's one thing to talk about becoming a celebrity in your field. It's quite another to actually begin the process. To make this book valuable to you – to make celebrity an authentic goal– we must first desensitize ourselves to the very word "celebrity."

The best place to start is to re-focus away from Hollywood or the Big Apple and turn it inward, toward yourself, your product, service, or expertise, and your industry.

Celebritizing yourself from the ground up brings to mind two of my favorite domestic goddesses turned celebrities: Julia Child and Erma Bombeck. I point to these two iconoclastic women because we're talking about specific industries, and these two virtually created their own. I suspect that you and I have a starting line much farther ahead than theirs was at the time of their burgeoning success.

Julia Child loved two things: French cooking and her husband, James (and, I suspect, sometimes in that order). Although Julia's background was in publicity and advertising, she single-handedly pursued her passion for French cooking with such expertise and zeal that no one around her could ignore. When she took to the airwaves of a small public television station back in 1963 to share her favorite French recipes with local Boston viewers, her star was born.

Julia became one of the first "celebrity chefs," and also one of the most recognizable women of the last century. She was not the traditional celebrity we think of today. Large, boisterous, and "handsome" at best, she hardly fit the cookie-cutter mold that typifies today's strong, independent female celebrities.

Nonetheless, she did one thing and did it well. So well, in fact, that she became the "go-to" person for everything culinary for many years. Such celebrity chefs as today's Emeril Lagasse and Rachel Ray owe their television careers to the pioneering efforts of Julia Child, as does the network that employs them: The Food Network. Truly, Julia is a poster child for how to become a celebrity in your own industry first, and then for the world at large.

So was Erma Bombeck. Dayton, Ohio born, Bombeck graduated from the University of Dayton in 1949 with a degree in English. She started her career that same year as a reporter for the *Ohio Journal Herald,* but after marrying school administrator Bill Bombeck, a college friend, she left the job to raise three children.

As her children grew, she wrote *At Wit's End,* a self-deprecating tale about the life of a housewife. Seen first in the *Kettering-Oakwood Times* in 1964, Emma was paid a miserly $3 per column.

The popularity of *At Wit's End* brought national syndication in 1965, and eventually it ran twice a week in more than 700 newspapers. The column was collected in many bestselling books, and her fame was such that a television sitcom was based on Erma's life. A humble $3 a column gig for the local paper graduated Erma to full celebrity status.

Today, the names of both women are synonymous with their professions. What's most inspiring about their stories is that even at the height of their fame, both women kept their perspective and they avoided the pitfalls so many other celebrities typically succumb to on the rise to power.

"Celebrity" for these two icons grew not out of ambition or greed – though both women clearly had business savvy and realized the far greater audience fame could bring to them. What they became famous *for* was what they loved. Their passion turned into "celebrity" which, in turn, added "celebrity" to their passion.

There is a strong lesson in here for all of us…

Celebritize Yourself Fact:

"Re-focus away from Hollywood or the Big Apple and turn it inward, toward yourself, your product, service, or expertise, and your industry."

A Million Fields – And a Celebrity for Each

Our first two celebrities prove that a star can truly rise to prominence in any field. Both women pioneered fame from their chosen professions. Before Julia Child, there were few celebrity chefs. Before Erma Bombeck, few newspaper columnists became best-selling book authors. Now both achievements are quite common. You might even say that book authorship is a requirement to celebritize oneself in those or in any other field.

So what about you? Since you're reading this you're probably ready to take that next step (though I doubt you'll have to invent a category as did Julia and Erma). I bet you can put your personal stamp on some already-existing field that can benefit from what you can tell your niche audience.

Congratulations! Finding a niche audience is the basic ingredient for the modern-day celebrity. Think of a field, any field, and I can name you a celebrity – if not a handful – that emerged from that same industry. There are the obvious names: real estate gave us Donald Trump; Vegas hospitality, Steve Wynn; Computers, Bill Gates; General Electric, Jack Welch.

But what about the not-so-obvious career fields? Being a handyman may not seem glamorous, yet it paid off handsomely for Kaile Warren, whose brainchild, "Rent-A-Husband", has garnered him national acclaim. If you think cleaning companies are not exactly a hotbed for workers-turned-celebrities, don't tell that to Linda Cobb. Before becoming nationally-recognized as "The Queen of Clean," Linda's cleaning firm tackled some of the most difficult cleaning tasks in the industry: disaster restoration, fire damage and smoke and water damage. And there was probably a story to tell behind each job!

There are some fields that no one could ever predict would birth celebrities. And yet we have Duane "Dog" Chapman, arguably the most famous bounty hunter alive thanks to his show on A&E. Then there's Linda Greenlaw, a swordfishing boat captain-turned-author. Her bestseller, *The Hungry Ocean,* is just her latest in a string of popular books that have given new blood to an occupation long overlooked. Used-car salesman turned-author, Lawrence Donegan, published *California Dreaming: A Smooth-Running, Low Mileage, Best-Priced American Adventure,* based upon his short-lived, but successful career as a used car salesman in San Jose, California.

What about your field? When I say any industry is ripe for a celebrity, I mean ANY. In my many years of promoting authors,

I've worked with experts from almost every field imaginable. Early in my career, one gentleman with a newly-published book wanted my help to get publicized. When he told me it was about how to make big money as a professional waiter, I thought for sure I had at last seen everything.

Turns out it was a great book on how to "turn tables," keep your customers happy, and make good money. The author, a consummate professional waiter, filled the book with great advice for restaurateurs.

Still another client had a book written by his 12-year-old son called, *Everything You Wanted Your Parents to Know, But Were Too Afraid To Tell Them.* He had great advice for parents. One such tidbit was how to act at your children's baseball or soccer game (no yelling allowed!) so as not to embarrass them. At the time, my young son was in Little League baseball. He never told his dad and me how he felt when Dad would yell from the stands to cheer him on. We were so appreciative of this young author's advice!

Another client wrote a book on *How to Kill Your Wife.* Okay, I'm being a little tongue-in-cheek here. But the book was a true story written by a well-educated man who was overtaken with rage after finding his wife in bed with another man. He killed her, went to prison for 25 years, and while in prison became an ordained Episcopalian Minister.

He now runs a widely popular church near Washington, D.C. helping newly released prisoners adjust back into society so they might live an honest life with the hope never to return to prison. There's a "how-to" book for you!

Hope I made my point?

When it comes to being a celebrity, any field of expertise WILL do.

Celebritize Yourself Fact:

"Think of a field, any field, and I can name you a celebrity – if not a handful –that emerged from that same industry."

So Who Wants to Be a Celebrity?

The reason I try so hard to hammer home the importance of becoming a celebrity in your field is because I've seen, firsthand, the benefits it can provide to one's self-esteem, business and finances.

Becoming a celebrity is no longer a mere luxury or "pie-in-the-sky" pipe dream. In our media-saturated world of high hopes and high-tech, it is nothing less than a prerequisite for success. I have personally watched clients skyrocket from industry nobody to industry leader based only on their celebrity status. What I find most interesting about these clients-turned-celebrities is that "I knew them when..."

One client was a personal trainer and local talk show host who had written a new book on fitness. He was well-known locally because of his radio show and gym, but this client had larger goals in mind. Thanks to his strong desire to become a nationally-recognized fitness expert, he became a household name in the '90s with the #1 selling diet and exercise infomercial.

Yes, "I knew him when...."

Often, very little changes from one's pre-celebrity days, yet one thing always changes: perception. The perception of those who now meet them, see them as celebrities versus mere coaches, CEO's, front-line managers or thought leaders.

When you celebritize yourself within your industry you gain instant credibility. Let's face it, celebrities are known, they're recognized. Rightly or wrongly, they are also more trusted. It's only human nature to believe in someone we see on television, hear on radio or read about in magazines and newspapers.

Fifteen politicians can debate a topic based on research, experience, and more research. It matters little how many awards they may have won, how many college degrees line their wall, or how much time they've actually spent investigating their particular topic. Yet, if one single celebrity says the same thing (regardless of its accuracy), we listen more closely, nod more firmly and believe more thoroughly.

This is instant cache. It's what I call the "commodity of celebrity," and is your greatest ally. It legitimizes your cause, lends credibility and, above all, gets your message heard. When celebrities speak, people listen! It's one of life's few remaining truisms.

So start to form your message now. We'll get into the specifics of that message later, but it's never too early to start distilling your message. In fact, the sooner the better. So often, people are eager to talk about everything they know from their industry expertise, but what they know easily gets distorted by over-telling. Focus on only what is important to say.

There is nothing worse than attaining local or national celebrity status and then finding yourself with so much to say that you end up saying nothing notable at all. There is one reason celebrities make fame look so easy; they work at it. Every day, all day. Their message is carefully rehearsed, analyzed, refocused, and rehearsed again.

Celebrities speak in sound bites, not because it comes naturally to them (although eventually, it must), but because they are *trained* to speak in sound bites. With enough practice, it can become automatic to keep comments to a few meaningful sentences. Not only is their appearance well-groomed; celebrities also groom their tailor-made message for mass consumption.

So, here is where OUR work starts: allow yourself to see how important you are and how important it is to celebritize yourself in today's crowded marketplace. Your knowledge and expertise is only as important as the reason you choose to offer it. It isn't enough to want to be a celebrity. To attain the commodity of celebrity, you must have a reason to do so.

Celebritize Yourself Fact:

"In our media-saturated world of high hopes and high tech, celebrity is nothing less than a prerequisite for success."

Celebrity Can Be a Life-Changer

So what CAN celebrity status do for you? A better question is what CAN'T it do? Seriously, though, becoming a national or even local celebrity in your industry *can* be a life changer. Celebrity is a powerful commodity; doors once closed, suddenly open. People listen to what they ignored before. Money flows to you – not away from you. Most of all, people thank you for sharing your wisdom.

Such is the essence of celebrity...

But, there are other perks you can look forward to:

- **Access**: Celebrities get invited past those velvet ropes into the V.I.P. lounge. Speaking engagements open, as do radio and TV interviews, and journalists actually return your phone calls. That is, if they don't pick up on the first ring! As someone who has personally waged battle with her share of gatekeepers over the past few decades, I can tell you that access alone is reason enough to become a celebrity.

- **Identity**: Anonymity can be boring. By assuming an identity as an expert in your field, as a celebrity, you elevate your position in life. It's about branding – and best of all, YOU control your own brand.

- **Credibility**: Celebrity means people agreeably nod their heads when you talk. They trust what you have to say. They buy in to the notion that hearing what a celebrity has to say is incredible. Audiences become willing participants in learning and sharing your message, automatically establishing your position as an opinion leader in your field.

- **Buy In:** That becomes your ticket to viral marketing on a grand scale. Becoming a celebrity is the fuse that ignites a chain reaction of collateral events that all reflect positively on you and your message. Think about the last good book you read, seminar you attended, or guest speaker you heard. Didn't you bounce back into the office on Monday morning anxious for the opportunity to tell someone about it?

Celebritize Yourself Fact:

"By assuming an identity as an expert in your field, as a celebrity, you elevate your position in life."

Best of All – You Help People

What is the value of a pulpit if you have nothing to say?

Becoming a celebrity in today's world is a privilege, not a right. It doesn't automatically happen. Many people contribute to the making of a celebrity. Beyond, and more important than the speaker, are those who listen. Beyond those who listen are those who create the venue to speak, the stage to speak on and the pulpit or podium to speak from. Many behind-the-scenes people create celebrities. It is the rare celebrity who can take sole credit for his or her own creation.

No matter what our field of expertise, once we gain ground as a celebrity, it's a great opportunity to use our status and recognition to better humanity. I don't mean to imply that we should all strive to be Mother Teresa; far from it. Still, we each have individual, unique attributes and specific qualities as the foundation of our fame.

We must be mindful of delivering a worthwhile message once given the opportunity. Again, this works for every field, every time. Rare is the celebrity who attains fame, and doesn't take up some worthy cause or share a worthwhile message.

When that message becomes part and parcel of the celebrity's brand, it fortifies both the message *and* the celebrity who delivers it. Bono has long been known for his charitable work. His efforts to end the world of poverty and hunger come as no surprise to either his legions of fans or the casual music listener.

The late Isaac Hayes worked to improve world literacy. Katie Couric is synonymous with promoting cancer screening. Wendy's founder, Dave Thomas, himself a foster child, was a strong supporter for raising awareness of the plight of foster children, and an advocate for child adoption. Dan Millman, author of *The Way of the Peaceful Warrior,* is largely credited with bringing Zen into vogue.

Tiger Woods' unwritten message of grace under pressure is evident both on and off the golf course. And, under the leadership of legendary CEO Jack Welch, General Electric reinvented itself several times over by integrating new and innovative practices into its many lines of business.

What about you? You've seen what celebrity can do for you. But still, one nagging question remains: What can YOU do for celebrity?

Celebritize Yourself Fact:

"We each have our individual, unique attributes and specific qualities as the foundation of our fame."

Wrapping Up: The Celebrity Commitment

As this chapter ends, I'll ask one final question: are you ready to commit to becoming a celebrity in your field? As I've said before, it takes far more than just the desire to be famous to become a celebrity.

More than charisma, more than charm, more than a message, a platform, a new wardrobe, and even more than stamina; celebrity requires commitment.

Without commitment, good intentions mean nothing. In the next chapter, we will discuss WHY you want to be a celebrity, but right now, ask yourself one vital question: Are you ready to become a celebrity?

If you enthusiastically answer yes, then I can't wait to show you where that exciting journey leads next…

Celebritize Yourself Fact:

"It takes far more than just the desire to be famous to become a celebrity."

Chapter 3:

Why Do You Want to Become a Celebrity?

"A life without fame can be a good life,
but fame without a life is no life at all."

~ Clive James (www.Thinkexist.com.)

I'm glad to see that you're still with me. Congratulations! That means you've made the celebrity commitment and are now ready for the next leg of your journey. Actually, this is my favorite part of the trip because it all starts from within. Here is where we take a good, hard look in the mirror. Here is where we get to know ourselves a whole lot better.

First, though, a few more questions: Why DO you want to become a celebrity? What's in it for you? What's your endgame? How will you "pay yourself" when all is said and done?

I think for most of us the answer is, quite simply, "having a purpose and achieving a goal." *American Heritage Dictionary* defines **purpose** as, "The object toward which one strives or for which something exists; goal; aim, etc."

A second definition is, "Determination; resolution..."

This chapter discusses the various purposes and personal reasons that motivate most people to want to become an acclaimed expert. Fame? Fortune? Career advancement? Longevity? More business? All reasons are right. It's only important to know your goals because they will help you to achieve your specific, unique and very personal reason to celebritize yourself.

This chapter encourages another question: do you have the passion to become a celebrity? It's not an easy path. And, as with running a marathon, it requires more than great running shoes and superior training. Potential celebs must have an insatiable drive, an inner sense of passion about their message, product, service, AND themselves in order to reach celebrity status.

Indeed, it's not for everyone...

Celebritize Yourself Fact:

*"American Heritage Dictionary defines **purpose** as: "The object toward which one strives or for which something exists; goal; aim, etc."*

5 Reasons Why I Want to be a Celebrity In My Field

From reading this book thus far, you're closing in on the "when" question. I already gave you the "what." You certainly know "who." Now it's time for "why." Specifically, write the top-5 reasons why YOU want to be a celebrity:

1. _____

2. _____

3. _____

4. _____

5. _____

But Is It For YOU?

At the end of the day, only one person can decide whether or not you should even attempt to become a celebrity. Not surprisingly, that person is YOU. Yet many people don't choose this path because they don't think their knowledge or expertise will be valued by others or that they have anything worthwhile to "share".

When my daughter was a young teenager I would compliment her drawings and poetry. She would say, "Oh, Mom, anyone can do that." I would assure her, "Not true – I can't!" Of course, she thought I was just being a loving mom. She never understood that her art and poetry were indeed very special. Unfortunately she didn't live long enough to understand the gift she could have shared with others.

The bottom line: there are many reasons not to step up to the "celebrity" plate, and, sadly, those reasons conquer many who try. Some ask, "Will people really like me? Will anyone come to this seminar or that conference? Will a busy, high-profile editor really return my calls? Will listeners call in if I go on the radio?"

Those new to the game of celebrity may think we can't control these situations, but the experienced celebrity knows this is untrue. It's simply a matter of IF and WILL:

- *If* you are an interesting guest, people *will* listen and producers *will* invite you back on the show.

- *If* you have a message, editors *will* answer the phone.

- *If* your article is good, newspapers, periodicals and Web sites *will* publish it.

The common denominator to each of those "ifs"? YOU.

Never let uncertainty overshadow your goals and purpose. You're obviously committed to becoming a celebrity or you wouldn't still be on this journey with me. Now, you must commit to something – or someone – even more important than the goal of celebrity, and that's you. The celebrity we're talking about here must come from somewhere deep inside you. Whether it's for money, popularity, or attention alone, you might achieve celebrity, but you surely won't *stay* a celebrity without the commitment to remain one.

The commitment, desire, and discipline required to achieve fame must be exceeded by the commitment, desire, and discipline needed to *sustain* fame. Vanity and greed are simply not enough to keep you on the top of the heap forever.

So dig deeper for the true reasons why you seek celebrity. Ask, "What sustains you? What drives you? What satisfies you? What fires you?" Your motives fuel the engine that drives celebrity.

For your engine to keep chugging along when times are tough, the public sentiment changes, or your industry shifts, you must be centered and extremely focused on achieving and sustaining your dreams.

Celebritize Yourself Fact:

*"The commitment, desire, and discipline required to **achieve** fame must be exceeded by the commitment, desire, and discipline needed to **sustain** fame."*

Five Signals That You're Ready for Celebrity

Have you ever watched a new star explode upon the public? Have you ever looked at someone and thought, "Man, where did they come from?" Have you ever heard yourself say, "I am soooooooooo taken with so and so..."? That, my friends, is the phenomena of overnight celebrity. The problem is, for most of us, celebrity status doesn't happen overnight.

There was a time "Before Dr. Phil" (BDP), when it was possible to watch TV, listen to the radio, visit a Web site, stroll through a bookstore or browse Amazon.com and NOT see that telltale chrome dome and bushy moustache. So exactly when did Dr. Phil's "overnight success" happen?

From curiosity I checked the copyright date of Phil's first book and, amazingly, it was as recent as 2001! In only a few short years, the man went from being at the top of his professional field to being second only to his mentor and benefactor, Oprah. Talk about being ready for celebrity!

Of course, the man paid his dues (and then some). By rising to the top of his profession, he was at the right place when opportunity (otherwise known as Oprah) came knocking.

But how will you know when it's your time to open the doorway to fame? Here are a few top signals that you're ready for that next big step toward your own brand of celebrity:

1. **You awaken in the middle of the night excited about your future:** One sign that you're ready to commit to celebrity is the simmering possibility that keeps you awake and energized. Celebrity is exciting. When you are excited about the possibility of spreading your message to thousands or millions of people, you're ready to take that next vital step.

2. **You can't stem the flow of new ideas:** When it comes to celebrity, few things are as valuable as ideas. We often talk of movers and shakers as "idea people." What we are really saying is that, unlike most of us, they have tapped into their inner spigot of ideas and refused to turn it off. Sounds like a plan to me!

3. **Your new mantra is, "I could do that, only better":** Future celebrities see opportunity everywhere. In particular, they can't abide mediocrity, especially in other "celebrities." When you start realizing that you are just as good, if not better, than others who are in vaulted celebrity positions, you're ready to have that spotlight shine on you.

4. **You find yourself prepping for fame:** If there's one thing Americans know about, it's celebrities. From press clippings to paparazzi, we are inundated with a culture of celebrity (whether or not we like it). When you begin thinking in sound bites, interviewing yourself, or searching for where to get the best "headshots" in town, you know you're ready for your shot at stardom.

5. **The only place to go is up:** Forget lateral moves. In today's world, the only way to go is up. And if you're already there, then you're ready to rise even further.

Celebritize Yourself Fact:
"When it comes to celebrity, few things are as valuable as ideas."

Celebrity By The Numbers

In most things, timing is everything. When it comes to celebrity, however, you hold the stopwatch! But before you can decide "when," you first need to decide "why". Why do YOU want to be a celebrity? The answer is not why I think it's a good idea for you. It's not why your colleagues want you to be the face that people recognize when they think of your company, product, or idea. It's not why your mother says it's such a good idea. It's all about YOU!

Celebritize Yourself Fact:

"In most things, timing is everything. When it comes to celebrity, however, you hold the stopwatch!"

Don't Wait for the Opportunity – Create It!

In later chapters, we will talk about the various steps you'll need to take to create your own celebrity. There is no mystery here; they are all fairly simple, highly accessible, and ultimately doable. The wild card will always be you. More specifically:

- What do **you** have to say?
- Why do **you** want to put yourself out there as a celebrity?
- How badly do **you** want it?
- How much effort are **you** willing to put into it?
- When will **you** be ready?

Let's focus on that last question. Many of us wait. And we wait. And we wait some more. We wait for inspiration. We wait for creativity. Worst of all, we wait for opportunity. Yet opportunity has no birth date, though it most definitely has an expiration date.

Unfortunately, too many of us let a great opportunity vanish for a variety of reasons: we're too busy, fearful, preoccupied, or we have poor funding; you name the excuse, I've heard it. You become a celebrity by recognizing a great opportunity or you make one where there was none. It's that basic!

Let me tell you more about the story of my friend Ben. He is a great example of creating an opportunity when there was none. It all started for him in the late '80s when he had a serious motorcycle accident. There was a mountain of unpaid medical bills and debt collectors out for the kill (with my friend as their main target). Never one to be down for the count, Ben learned about debt collections and his legal rights as a debtor.

After paying off his debts (and nearly killing off the collectors), he wrote a bestselling book to help others harassed by debt collectors. But the opportunity that he created didn't stop there. After doing hundreds of radio shows to promote his book, he wound up with his own radio show, made frequent appearances on nationally syndicated TV shows, became a columnist for a major daily newspaper in a top US market and a regular contributor to two major network morning TV shows. Talk about creating an opportunity where there was none! My friend Ben is a master.

I can tell you this much about the celebrities I've worked with: they don't wait for opportunity. They create their own. I urge you to invite this good habit into the fold. Be constantly on the lookout for opportunities to speak, write, share, post or even email people about what you're doing. If you start to feel that no such opportunities exist, just look harder for ways to create them.

This chapter is all about the WHY of celebrity. The sooner you discover WHY you want to become a celebrity, the more you will be motivated to create the opportunity.

Celebritize Yourself Fact:

"Opportunity has no birth date, though it most definitely has an expiration date."

The Most Important Question: Why Not?

I often encourage people to think about "why" they should become a celebrity, "why" I think it's right for them, "why" I think they're right for celebrity and, most importantly, "why" it will help them, their business, their credibility and their income.

But, more and more often, I also ask why not? Why NOT become a celebrity? In other words, what do you have to lose? The steps that it takes to add credibility and celebrity to your life are small, but significant. Often these steps will help your business anyway by increasing your visibility. Publishing articles, courting the press, getting your message heard on the radio, and appearing on TV adds value to you and your business. The floodgates can open up. Clients can pour in. After all, the word is out that you're the best in the business!

Such promotional efforts are no longer tools for the loud and energetic only; they are also tools for the stalwart and serious. If you are expecting to do business in the next five or ten years (and who isn't?), you must inevitably do those things anyway.

More and more, the world seeks brands. Don't like that buzzword? Try "identity," "distinction," "visibility" or "recognition" - call it what you will. The endgame is the same: people buy from whom – or what – they know. More often, they ONLY buy from whom – or what – they know.

We've seen this in retail with the popularity of Wal-Mart and Target. (Seriously, when's the last time you visited a mom-and-pop retail store?) We've seen it on the Web with Amazon.com, eBay and Google. We've seen it in entertainment as CD sales plummet while iPods soar.

The world is changing, particularly when it comes to how – and even where – we communicate. It is no longer only a matter of what we say, but how many people hear us say it.

So don't ask yourself, "Why should I become a celebrity?" Ask yourself, "Why not?"

Celebritize Yourself Fact:

"The steps that it takes to add credibility and celebrity to your life are small, but significant."

Chapter 4:
First, Know Thyself

"Love yourself first and everything else falls into line. You really have to love yourself to get anything done in this world."

~ Lucille Ball

America's favorite redhead was right: it's all about loving yourself. In our case, we just need to change the "love" part to "know." Actually, the words are quite similar. As the saying goes, "To know thyself is to love thyself." Now we just need to get the rest of the world to know you – and love you – too!

At its heart, this chapter talks about discovering what you're an expert at. "Knowing yourself" is all about having a passion to share that knowledge, and then celebritizing it. It is a process, but over and above the nuts and bolts of that process, there must be that underlying sense of passion and commitment to the process.

You must know yourself to express yourself.

Consider this a motivational chapter. It will help you mine your inner dreams, secrets and desires. It will bring out that sense of passion before you hone in on where your celebrity status will occur. It's not as easy as simply saying "I want to be famous" and then putting in the time and effort to achieve it. To pull off something as bold and iconic as name brand identity, you can't just have the name and the brand; you must first have the identity.

Identity boils down to simply this: who knows you? Is it only your family and friends, employees, colleagues, coaches, or clients? Your banker, doctor, broker, or fitness trainer? To all these people you have an identity.

Identity is no more or less complicated. Here the question becomes, "If you call yourself a celebrity but no one knows who you are, will they listen?" Unfortunately, the answer is clearly, "No."

Once you truly know yourself, your public identity becomes an extension of who you really are. Many of us have trouble firming up our identity because we're still trying to figure out what we want to be when we grow up! But celebrities, good or bad, have very clear public identities. Case in point: If we play the "If I say **this,** you think of **that**..." game about any celebrity, their famous status quickly boils down to one or two words.

For instance, when I mention Oprah Winfrey, most people immediately respond with words such as, "driven," "passionate," and "dedicated." This successful TV personality is known to be compassionate and caring about people. She's dedicated to causes that improve people's lives and she's driven by success. Conversely, mention Paris Hilton, and people may just as quickly respond with opposite terms - "vapid," "pampered" and "spoiled."

How will **you** be known?

You'll never know until you truly *know* yourself.

Many celebrities consciously brand themselves in a way that is almost too calculated to seem sincere. I think Martha Stewart falls into this category. Her success may have been a "good thing" for her, but in interviews, on her show and in personal appearances, she comes off as less of a person and more of a product.

On the other hand, the *Today Show's* Matt Lauer has a more positive, personable identity as an unassuming, self-effacing reporter. He is known for being passionate about his personal and professional life that seemingly intertwines. Two instantly recognizable celebrities; two very different identities.

Identity. It all boils down to having an expertise, believing unequivocally that your knowledge is valuable to others, and having the passion (for whatever reason) to share that knowledge.

I'm reminded of a business trip to Colorado when I sat next to a gentleman on the plane who started a conversation about the speech notes I had been working on. (Apparently, he was reading over my shoulder!) Fascinated with my work as a publicist, he wanted to know what I could do for him. I discovered that he was a financial planner on his way to a marketing convention.

I told him, as I'm telling you, that step one is – write a book. His response (and one I get frequently), "I don't write, I teach. Moreover, there are already tons of books out there on financial planning." It took a while for him to believe that HIS book could be far different than anything on the market since it would carry his unique message.

We talked for an hour, crystallizing what that message was. I probed with questions about his expertise and how I would benefit if I hired him as my financial advisor. He gave me his standard sales pitch. Finally, I asked him how he was different from other financial planners, what aspect of financial planning was he passionate about, what did he spend his time reading and researching, etc.

Only when he announced his passion was for the special financial plights of the "suddenly single" did we know we hit gold in terms of a topic for his book. It was an introspective process that helped him to understand more about himself. And what a great jumpstart for the marketing convention he was attending. He got his money's worth on that plane ride!

The moral of the story is: whether we are a doctor, a lawyer, a car mechanic, a waiter or plumber, we each excel at something. To identify that "something" enables you to *Celebritize Yourself.*

You might be an "entrepreneur extraordinaire" with a business you built from nothing that's now worth millions. A girlfriend of mine did just that. Her direct mail marketing company was recently recognized in *Inc. Magazine's* famous list of 500 Fastest Growing Companies.

Perhaps you've discovered a way someone can achieve their hidden dream. Another friend of mine developed a technology that can teach anyone to sing! Or maybe you once weighed 300 pounds and, after years of failed dieting, you've finally figured out the magical formula to lose weight and keep it off!

Perhaps you've been married for 30 years and have the most wonderful relationship with your spouse – the kind that movies are made of and great love songs are written about. Or, it could be that you've raised healthy, happy children who are now productive members of society and are raising your grandchildren with the same principles!

Perhaps you were a teacher who brought out the best in your students, many of whom went on to achieve great success because of your caring ways. Whatever your passion, whatever your purpose, this chapter is about finding it, honing it and achieving it!

Okay, so you've figured out what you're terrific at. It's now time for everyone else to know the expert within you!

Celebritize Yourself Fact:

*"How will **you** be known? You'll never know until you truly **know** yourself."*

Top 5 Things I'd Like to Change About the World

So, what are you dissatisfied with? What would you like to change? Here's your chance to explore those feelings and pin them down with specific answers:

1. _____

2. _____

3. _____

4. _____

5. _____

Overcome Your Obstacles

Part and parcel of knowing yourself is coming to terms with who you are, warts and all. Don't just look in the mirror when the light is just right or your makeup's perfect. See yourself for who you really are when no one's looking and your guard is down. This is not a time for resume-fluffing, masking or denial.

Rather, this is an opportunity for you to come face-to-face with who you really are, what you're all about and, why, oh why, you want to sign up for this long tour of duty on the way to celebrity. Trust me, it's better to come clean with yourself now, rather than later. You have a real chance here to speak to your authentic self and open up a dialogue that perhaps you've never engaged in before.

In sections to come, we will discuss your strengths, weaknesses, passions and desires. Right now I'd like to discuss what you don't want; what you're dissatisfied with about yourself. Many of us come to celebrity wanting – or needing – to change things for the better.

We want to right a wrong, cure an ill, or perhaps just stop a growing trend leading us in a wrong direction. For instance, my business clients often write about how they want to revolutionize their industry; my motivational clients talk about changing the way we think about ourselves to achieve our goals; my health and fitness clients want to end the rising tide of obesity that seems to be sweeping the country.

Clearly, it's the desire to improve conditions that drives people as much as anything else. Like the client who recently told me, "I'm not so sure about what I want to achieve, but I sure know what I want to change about the world if given the opportunity!"

Celebritize Yourself Fact:

"Many of us come to celebrity wanting – or needing – to change things for the better."

Unleash Your Desires

Feel better? Good! Because now it's time to switch gears and talk about what you want, as opposed to what you want to change. Oftentimes, the two go hand in hand. For instance, if you don't want violence, you naturally want peace; if you don't want mediocrity, you want success. But there's a difference between what you merely "want" and what you *desire.*

Being passionate about something is "want" personified; passion is what "want" becomes when it grows up!

There was a show on VH-1 called *Driven* that really spoke to the difference between want and desire. I wasn't a diehard fan of the actual series, but the few episodes I watched always left me more informed about what makes someone merely "want to be" a celebrity and what makes others actually realize their goals and *become* a celebrity.

To be sure, it's easy to poke fun at the recent rash of reality TV stars turned celebrities. Pick a winner, or even a loser, from Donald Trump's hit series, *The Apprentice,* and you'll find him or her hawking a bestseller at the local Barnes & Noble. At a time when record sales are slumping with brick and mortar music stores closing left and right, reality TV stars like Kelly Clarkson and Carrie Underwood are among the few thriving singers still selling platinum CDs.

Reality TV stars seek celebrity. They aren't just picked at random off the streets or spotted in coffee shops then given million dollar contracts.

In fact, today's reality stars go through an intense and rigorous selection process that requires reams of paperwork, auditions, interviews, callbacks and more interviews. (Hmm, kind of sounds to me like what "real" stars go through.) Those who make it to the top of the heap don't just want celebrity, they're passionate about it. They are, in a word, *driven*.

You remember Rupert, the most favored contestant from the successful TV reality show, *Survivor?* I recently met Rupert at a dinner where he was giving a speech about troubled kids. Unbeknownst to many, he has a non-profit foundation called "Rupert's Kids" and his desire for celebrity is about helping teenagers "in the system" turn their life around. We'll be hearing a lot more about Rupert, I'm sure.

Why? Because he's driven.

Celebritize Yourself Fact:

"Being passionate about something is 'want' personified; passion is what 'want' becomes when it grows up!"

Identify Your Strengths

No inward journey is complete without exploring your strengths and weaknesses, so in these next two sections we'll cover both at length. For starters, I always begin with strengths. Why? Because for one thing, it's much easier for people to talk about what they're good at than what they're not so good at.

But more importantly, your true strengths are what most people will see and come to admire about you.

So what do you bring to the table? Are your speaking skills an asset? Is your personal charm a blessing? Can you think on the fly? Do you play well with others?

It sometimes seems difficult to assess your own assets, but not really, if you're willing to be honest with yourself. More then ever before, now is the time to really examine things about yourself that you may never have looked at before. What do you do best? Of all the things you do, what do you enjoy most? Those are your strengths and it's time to hone in on them. But don't just recognize them – enhance them, embrace them and celebrate them.

Celebritize Yourself Fact:

"...your true strengths are what most people will see and come to admire about you."

My Top-5 Strengths

Now, it's time to look at your own strengths in the following test. Identify them so they can shine.

1. _____

2. _____

3. _____

4. _____

5. _____

Also Spot Your Weaknesses

Now that we know what makes you so strong, we come to the more difficult part: recognizing your weaknesses! Please take this section seriously. I really do want you to be honest with yourself here, so I add this quick caveat: weaknesses are not the same as faults. Often we confuse the two, but, in fact, recognizing our weaknesses, and correcting them, can turn them into strengths in time.

Case in point: one friend was a poor public speaker who fumbled his words and messed up every speaking engagement. It wasn't only embarrassing; it also hurt his income opportunities. But he really believed he was a great public speaker! He had more confidence as a poor speaker than most good public speakers have in their far more accomplished presentations.

Well, confidence is a key to celebritizing yourself, however, in this case, it was a locked door keeping my friend out of the millionaire's club! Eventually, as business decreased from one year to the next, I urged my friend to confront his greatest "strength" and see it for the weakness it really was.

Only when he fully realized the wide gap between his perception and reality could my friend truly tackle his speaking weakness. He practiced diligently. How often did he say "uh" or "you know" in a presentation? How often did he fail to make eye contact? He worked on his voice, posture, stage presence, and even his dress.

No, it was not a miraculous transformation; nor did it happen overnight. It was a slow, deliberate and complete metamorphosis over time. With practice, commitment, and most of all under-standing the need for correction, his biggest weakness became his biggest strength.

5 Weaknesses That Must Change

Hone in on what you feel are the biggest weaknesses you need to change.

1. _____

2. _____

3. _____

4. _____

5. _____

Celebritize Yourself Fact:

"Weaknesses are not the same as faults. Often we confuse the two, but, in fact, recognizing our weaknesses – and correcting them – can turn them into strengths in time."

What's So Different About You?

Our next – and final – two sections about getting to "know thyself" pinpoint what you're capable of investing into the celebrity process and what you're hoping to get out of it.

We talked earlier about identity. Now, let's follow-up that discussion by emphasizing the need to find that one unique quality about you. Let's reduce identity to its lowest common denominator. In other words: What do you have to offer? How do you differ from other experts in your field?

Celebrities abound these days in so many different fields. There is simply no room for mimics, rip-offs or carbon copies. Not only must you be yourself, but you must be yourself and then some!

It's a truly amazing and quite often confounding challenge. On the other hand, it's entirely necessary. Don't believe me? We've already characterized both Martha Stewart and Donald Trump; now let's talk about when they met. Remember when there used to be two *Apprentices?* One was Donald's version and another was Martha's. Guess whose won?

Of course, one had to go. There was room for Donald to be Donald and there was room for Martha to be Martha. But only one of them could be "the boss." Despite her considerable talents, Martha had too little clout to triumph over Donald's original *Apprentice.*

There is a lesson in this: no matter how much cache you have as a non-celebrity, the field becomes much tighter – and deadlier –

when you throw your hat into the volatile ring of celebrity. You must be bigger, tougher, stronger, smarter, louder, wiser and, above all, DISTINCTIVE.

There is room for many more experts who want to become celebrities. There are so many industries, so many new ideas, so much new technology - and every blog, newsletter, Web site, book, and philosophy introduces new and unique celebrities daily. But the key word is "unique."

A great example from many years ago is a client of mine, a famous cardiologist who wrote a book on heart disease. What made him truly unique were his unconventional ways to prevent heart disease. He prescribed a regimen of vitamins and diet. His methods are no longer unconventional, but I'm certain he greatly influenced the media and the public in regard to these emerging health trends.

What, specifically, can you bring to the table of celebrity? What is your unique message? If you are a cancer survivor interested in writing a book about fitness, what new and unique added value can you, as the author, bring to the reader? If you are a plastic surgeon doing keynotes on non-surgical procedures, what can you say that is different from what dozens of other cosmetic surgeons have already said on the subject?

Celebritize Yourself Fact:
"So not only must you be yourself, but you must be yourself and then some!"

---

5 Things Only I Can Bring to Celebrity

Finding something unique about yourself and what you have to tell is what qualifies you as unique. It is the first step. Scope out the competition. Find their common denominator. Separate yourself from them. Ready? Let's spot your unique quality:

1. _____

2. _____

3. _____

4. _____

5. _____

Name Your Own Rewards

Finally, we come to what you want to gain from celebrity. We've talked about what you must put in – hard work, a unique message, a revolutionary platform, etc. But now define what you want out of celebrity. Go beyond the monetary riches or fancier tables at nicer restaurants. What would be the **real payoff** for you?

In other words, what do you realistically expect to achieve by reaching celebrity status? Is it that your message will finally reach a large audience or any audience at all? Is it that people will benefit from your new invention, idea or technique? Will your businesses run better? Will people feel better?

Achieving your goals is certainly the ultimate reward, but it can only happen if you can define success in your own terms.

Celebritize Yourself Fact:
"Achieving your goals is certainly the ultimate reward, but it can only happen if you can define success in your own terms."

---

5 Things That I Want From Celebrity

Name your goals and the reward you want from it all! What will mean success to you?

1. _____

2. _____

3. _____

4. _____

5. _____

Know Yourself

So, how'd you do? I know it can be frustrating to peer so closely into the mirror, but I hope your journey paid off in more than just the obvious, feel-good ways.

Regardless of how it feels, I can say with utmost confidence that it's an entirely necessary process you must repeat over and over again through the course of your career as a celebrity.

Time marches on. People change. The "you" that you were yesterday is not necessarily the "you" of tomorrow. And this is good. As the old adage claims, "The moment you're through changing, you're through." But reinventing yourself will come later. Right now, let's just invent you. And, as we have seen, that requires truly knowing yourself.

Celebritize Yourself Fact:

"Time marches on. People change. The 'you' that you were yesterday is not necessarily the 'you' of tomorrow."

---

5 Things That I Now Know Better About Myself

Let's sum it up:

1. _____

2. _____

3. _____

4. _____

5. _____

Chapter 5:
It All Starts With a Book

"When I get a little money I buy books; and if any is left, I buy food and clothes."

~ Desiderius Erasmus

At the heart of the *Celebritize Yourself* process is a book. Why a book? The answer is simple: it's a tangible way to define "you" and your message. Most of my clients propel themselves to the next level simply by mentioning their own book.

Proudly showing a book cover, or sending prospects to find your book on Amazon.com (or at a brick and mortar bookstore in their locale), will always clinch a deal for the newly-published author. But let's take it to the next level – a book also opens the door to the media. And media is a pathway to the public you're trying to influence.

So what if the mere thought of writing a business plan or memo overwhelms you – let alone an entire book? Well, hold on. It has never been easier to hire a freelance writer, editor or even full-fledged ghostwriter to help turn your ideas into a book. Unbeknownst to most readers, a huge percentage of books are written with the help of professional writers. According to Gary McLaren, editor of *Worldwide Freelance Writer,* "Statistics are hard to come by since many people don't want to reveal that their book is ghosted. Some industry estimates suggest that up to fifty percent of all non-fiction books are ghostwritten."

So, don't worry if you don't see yourself as an "author." An entire industry of writers is there to help you, and a book is vital for a celebrity. This chapter reveals "how" to get your book written cost-effectively and expediently, especially if there's no writer within you. It also discusses the question of whether to self-publish or shop for a conventional publisher. Since this is a question I get asked quite often, I'll go into the pros and cons of each, based on the personal experiences of myself or my clients.

Celebritize Yourself Fact:

"A book also opens the door to the media. And media is the pathway to the public you're trying to influence."

Books: America's New Business Card

If you're still undecided about whether a book can propel you to celebrity status, consider a scene of two people who walk into your office each seeking your business. Each has impeccable credentials, is wearing a tailored suit, and has an impressive resume that sparkles with confidence and great talent. One candidate hands you a glossy business card. The second hands you his book.

Quickly: who just won your business?

Let's face it, in our business – in *any* business – it's all about perception. When we meet a book's author, we immediately perceive that person to be an expert on whatever subject he or she is writing about. That author is far more impressive than the guy or gal who comes along **without a book.**

For someone to take the time to write about a topic, give it an impressive title and subtitle, organize it, review it, plan it and get it published, says much about a person. It makes that person special and unique. It's an impressive credential.

It will do the same for you.

I tell you this because if you are ever to truly celebritize yourself, you must begin to think about yourself not just as a celebrity but as an expert-turned-author-turned-celebrity. Books are central to the *Celebritize Yourself* process.

A book gives you instant cache. It ups your credibility factor. To stay competitive in today's cutthroat world of would-be experts, a book is no longer a standout – it's a must-have.

Name almost any expert you can think of – in any field – and you will find them listed on Amazon.com. And not just in the music or DVD sections, but under books. You'll find thousands! Try it. You'll see my point. Today's book is yesterday's business card. It is an instant introduction to your thoughts, feelings, expertise, know-how, advice, wisdom, and personality, rolled into a neat 200-300 page package within a cover of credibility-boosting blurbs from respected peers and colleagues. Add your snappy author's photo, wrap it in a great title (and subtitle), create a slam-bang cover with your name on it and, presto-chango, you are now an author ready to compete on the same playing field as any other celebrity.

Now, all you have to do is come up with that great idea for a best-selling book that can magnetize an endless stream of clients or customers.

Celebritize Yourself Fact:

*"When we meet a book's author, we immediately perceive that person to be an expert on whatever subject he or she is writing about. That author is far more impressive than the guy or gal who comes along **without a book.**"*

Make Your Book Your Message

To win the game, you need more than a book. You need a great message – and a well promoted book! A poorly-conceived, poorly-titled, poorly-*written* or poorly promoted book is not much better than no book at all. Much as you build your future celebrity around a central theme, so too must your book revolve around that unique and worthy message that represents you. It becomes your brand.

Many people tell me, "You know, I always knew I had a book in me!" Unfortunately, if that book is a fiction thriller that has nothing to do with the field in which they are trying to become a celebrity, it won't help them to build their business. Don't get me wrong – fiction is a valuable form of writing, but when your goal is to become a celebrity in your specific field, every step you take – including the book you write – must move specifically toward the message you wish to convey.

For instance, if you are a successful, well-respected doctor hoping to celebritize yourself in the field of non-surgical cosmetic procedures, then your message – and your book – must be about one thing: non-surgical cosmetic procedures and how it can benefit prospective patients.

If you are a CEO hoping to become a keynote speaker on the topic of leadership, then your message – and your book – must be about one thing only: leadership. You must bring to that theme a unique message, twist, or angle.

Several years ago, a woman asked me to help her promote her novel about angels and spirituality. We'll call her "Terry" for the purpose of telling this story. I explained that it was <u>VERY</u> difficult to gain national exposure for novels, particularly for the unknown author. I did not want to thwart her enthusiasm, nor did I want to be a dream killer, so I dug a little deeper to discover Terry's true goal. Did she envision herself as a best-selling fiction author? Perhaps the next Marianne Williamson? Was she trying to raise public awareness about angels? Only by understanding Terry's objective, could I better guide her.

It turned out "none of the above" was really the answer. Terry's husband was diagnosed with cancer and she could foresee the financial and personal impact this would have on their business and their life. Terry loved to write and she thought a book would provide another source of income.

Once I learned that Terry owned her own business, I had something specific to work with. I knew I could help! I asked about her business (her specific role in the business), if she enjoyed her work, how she attracted clients, and so forth. Terry talked and I listened. This woman wanted my help and I would give it to her. There are few things that I enjoy more.

What I learned was that Terry was an expert landscape designer. Not only did she have a successful landscaping business, but she also loved to write! What a great combination of talent to create a unique business-building book! Terry had it all and didn't realize it.

I told Terry to bury the novel idea for now and instead write a 'how-to book' about landscape design. She asked, "Marsha, do you really think enough people would be interested in landscape design?"

I asked Terry how many people sought her expert opinion about how to enhance their yards. "Well, it happens every day," she admitted. Suddenly the bright lights went on. She told me how her clients relied on her advice to create beautiful gardens they once only dreamt about – and how she could view barren land much as an artist sees a blank canvas and then visualize just the right plants and trees to transform the land into a magnificent landscape.

Terry started to connect the dots. She loved writing and wanted more income as an author. She had professional expertise, a local service business, and walk-in traffic. Her formula was complete.

Terry could see that a book would be a wonderful marketing tool for her business and how it would also set her far above her competition. I discussed book promotion, explained how her book would open media doors for her, and described how she could soon gain local celebrity status (and lots of new business) as a top landscape designer.

Terry's story perfectly exemplifies why your message and your book must fit together. They should not be apples and oranges. If your message is to sell apples, your book must be about apples. If the goal of your message is to sell oranges, talk about oranges and why yours are the best.

To become a celebrity don't make fruit salad! Know what it is you're trying to sell – and write about it.

Celebritize Yourself Fact:

"Much as you build your future celebrity around a central theme, so too must your book revolve around that unique and worthy message that represents you. It becomes your brand."

To Succeed – Plan for Success

Now you know why you need a book to become a celebrity and why your book must match the message you want to convey. So, what's next? Planning. Plain and simple. Whether or not you decide to write the book yourself (we'll get to your options on this matter in a moment), the main idea of the book must come from within you. This is often the hardest part.

A book is more than printed words on a page. A book is an idea brought to life. Whose idea? Your idea. So, as the first part of our planning process, think about your idea by answering five basic questions:

1. What message am I enthusiastic about that I want to convey?
2. Who can benefit from it?
3. How will it help them?
4. Why am I the one to bring this idea to them?
5. How can I make my points unique and different from what has already been said on the topic by others?

Several ideas may be swimming in your head as you read this, as they were in mine before I wrote this book. That's fine; that's great. Give each idea a test drive. Write each idea on a piece of paper then answer the five questions for each specific idea. Do this and I guarantee you'll find the one idea that most lights your fire. It may be the idea you never realized you had such passion about.

Watch your own personal indicators. Which idea makes you smile? Which excites you creatively? Which idea hits the essence of what you're about – what you most enjoy, think about, and create daily?

Let me share another personal experience with you. I've been in the publicity business since 1990. Every day we develop winning angles and write press releases to secure national exposure for my clients on radio and TV, and get them coverage in newspapers and magazines. I talk to clients and prospective clients daily to get the right pitch and angle for maximum media exposure. I've talked to business groups and professional groups – and they always ask the same question: how can they get more media exposure for themselves or their business?

So, when the time came for me to figure out my message, it was natural for me to consider writing a "how-to" book to answer people's most common questions about publicity. In fact, I could with my eyes closed, so to speak! But when I actually sat down to write this book, I realized that it didn't pass my first criteria. It wasn't the message that I was most enthusiastic about. I tried to muster my enthusiasm, but it just wasn't happening.

If you've ever before attempted to write a book, you know the dedication you need to make it happen. I wasn't sufficiently enthused about that theme, so I knew there was no way I would find time in my already hectic life to actually sit down and write about it.

I have a thriving business with employees and clients who rely on me. I'm at my office nearly 24/7 and, when I'm not at the office, I'm at the radio station for my radio show and I'm at home wearing my other hats as wife and mother. Not to mention my time-consuming charitable activities. I knew enough about myself to know that if I wasn't highly enthusiastic about writing this book, it just wouldn't happen. But, how could I resolve this problem? How could I possibly guide others if I couldn't even guide myself?

As I went through this process, the answer seemed impossible. I mean, what else would I write about? Publicity and marketing is who I am; it's what I do. Of course, there were also a number of other good books on these topics already. So question 5 was my challenge. I asked myself, "What do I most enjoy about my professional life?"

The answer was easy. I love best to talk to people who are on a positive mission - those with a strong desire to help others and who want to get their word out but don't know how to make it happen. I love best to talk to people who are on a positive mission - those with a strong desire to help others and who want to get their word out but don't know how to make it happen.

You must "zero-in" on the one singular, unifying idea that excites and energizes you – the one that urges you to get out of bed every morning – the one that defines who you are and what you represent. This one central idea will be the driving force behind every single word within your book.

I recently spoke to two different authors. Both were highly educated and both were winding down their successful careers. One author was an MD; the other was a social worker/professor in gerontology. Both wanted me to help them promote their books. The doctor's book was on how to prevent children from abusing drugs and alcohol. Although this wasn't his major area of practice, nevertheless he counseled many of his patients and his own family members on drug abuse. He felt he could help parents detect and prevent their children from becoming addicted to drugs. The other author, a 60-year-old woman, wrote a book entitled, *Love and Sex: Are We Ever Too Old?*

Both authors had just passed the golden 60 mark. They wrote their books not because they wanted to change careers and make a living as best-selling authors, but because each saw their book as a defining moment in their lifetime. They had an important message, a message they needed to share. It was their way to "leave their mark."

Stop scratching your head! Yes, the thought of writing a book – even *planning* a book – can be a daunting task. But take my advice. Follow my 5-question guide in this chapter and you'll find your own unique message – I promise!

Celebritize Yourself Fact:
"A book is more than printed words on a page. A book is an idea brought to life."

Author! Author!

Writing a book is more than honing your message on a few hundred pages. When you write a book you become an author, and becoming an author makes you more credible in the eyes of those who are important to you – your friends, family, colleagues, peers, clients, coaches, mentors, audiences, and so forth.

Authorship makes you an expert. An expert in *what* is entirely up to you. Ben, the friend I spoke about earlier, became an expert in debt collection agencies. He wanted to combat their abuse tactics that almost brought him down – tactics that were unethical and – sometimes – illegal. That was Ben's defining message: don't get beaten down by debt collectors. Don't let them ruin your life. Part drill instructor and part hand holder, Ben's message never wavered.

People read his book, *Back Off: The Definitive Guide to Stopping Debt Collection Agency Harassment.* And they took notice. They associated Ben with those five words: *Stopping Debt Collection Agency Harassment.* Audiences heard him use that admonition time and again. Ben conducted speaking gigs, seminars, and his own radio talk show, plus he wrote a column for a major daily newspaper, Web site and newsletter.

This didn't happen because Ben nearly went bankrupt.

This didn't happen because Ben survived the system.

This happened because Ben made himself the expert on this topic. Ben became someone who beat the system and turned *author* then celebrity. His message and his book were simpatico. Ben made it easy for his readers to help themselves. They didn't shake their heads; they nodded in appreciation as they systematically solved their money problems following Ben's instructions.

The title *Debt Collection Agency Harassment* made people take notice. His title and tag-line had a compelling rhythmic flow. They implied power, action, and survival. They drew readers deeper into the book. His book's coherent message and "read-today-use-tomorrow" tips, steps, practices, and solutions were invaluable.

As a celebrity, Ben became many things: a consumer advocate, a media personality, and an author. Each role was no less important than the other. But his number one goal was to have a platform to help people with his knowledge and experience. His book was only one component of the total celebrity package and his journey to celebrity did not stop there.

This chapter is supremely important to getting the book written, because for many of us, the mere idea of writing a book is so daunting. But it is only one step.

The journey to celebrity is a journey with many requirements to reach the end point. Writing a book is only the first element. Becoming a <u>successful</u> author is another. Each step is vital.

If writing a book discourages your thoughts of becoming a celebrity, then read the next section carefully. It may have a solution for you.

Celebritize Yourself Fact:

"When you write a book you become an author, and becoming an author makes you more credible in the eyes of those who are important to you – your friends, family, colleagues, peers, clients, coaches, mentors, audiences, and so forth."

Do You Need a Little Writing Help With Your Book?

While most of us have plenty of good book ideas to keep us up at night, once morning strikes, the alarm clock rings, and the harsh light of reality smacks us in the face, not all of us have what it takes to actually write a book. That's when it makes sense to hire a professional ghostwriter who writes for a living.

Unbeknownst to most would-be celebrities, a thriving industry of editors, freelancers, ghostwriters, collaborators, co-authors, and consultants lurk behind the scenes, ready and willing to assist you. They do a thriving business by taking a good book idea from conception to completion.

As one ghostwriter exclaims, "From brainstorm to bestseller!"

If time is of the essence – and it usually is – then the six to twelve months it might take you to write your own book might be cut in half by a professional freelance writer who can deliver the bestseller you want.

For most of us, writing a book is a long and extensive process with a steep, unforgiving learning curve. As the fellow I met on the plane said when I told him he needed a book, "But I'm a researcher and public speaker - not a writer!" Perhaps he was right. Research, style and grammar, honing our ideas into coherent sentences, re-writing line after line and paragraph after paragraph, self-editing, and proofreading are all arduous tasks, to say the least.

A trained writing professional already knows proper punctuation and the rules of grammar. They can outline a book in their sleep; writing is their forte. There is no learning curve. They are already well-trained and well-prepared to work with clients like yourself to produce your ideal book.

Which is which? What's the difference between a copywriter and a collaborator? What does a ghostwriter do versus, say, an editor? Here is a quick and simple definition of their roles to help you determine whether you'd prefer to have some or even all the writing of your book handled by one of these freelancers.

- **Editor:** You'll need one even when you've written most of the book yourself. A qualified editor can fill in the gaps and polish what you've already created. Editors usually proofread the final manuscript for typos or other errors.

- **Copywriter:** Copywriters start where editors stop, penning original material that can be weaved into your own.

- **Ghostwriter:** A ghostwriter writes as much or little of the book as you desire. A good ghostwriter can take an idea from concept to completion and, with your creative input, create a polished, professional book in as little as 4-5 months.

- **Collaborator:** Some writing professionals prefer to get some credit for their work. These are "collaborators" not "ghostwriters," but they technically perform much the same function – to turn your ideas into a book as you might write it had you the inclination, time, or talent. But for the privilege of seeing their name alongside yours, they typically charge less than a ghostwriter.

- **Co-author:** From time to time, you can convince a ghostwriter/collaborator to become so enthusiastic about your idea that he or she might forego initial compensation and write the book with you, gratis, as a co-author. Or the two of you can negotiate to divide the proceeds from the book.

So how do you find these professionals to help you create your own powerful book? A variety of professional sites feature services where authors who require writers can post their needs and get bids from these "ghosts." Two particularly good sites are Guru.com and Elance.com. You can also Google; "ghostwriter," "copywriter" or "freelance writer" to reveal dozens more. Other "ghosts" advertise in both the print and online versions of *Writer's Digest Magazine,* and on www.craigslist.com.

How much will their services cost you? The answer depends on what they do for you. Professional ghostwriters might charge between $5,000 and $20,000 to shape your rough book idea into a complete, full-fledged, camera-ready book. Editors, collaborators and copywriters usually charge $15 to $45 per hour. These costs aren't cheap, but they are good investments if you truly want to achieve future celebrity but can't quite churn out a good book entirely on your own.

If a speaking engagement pays $2,500, for example, you see that you can pay for your ghostwriter with only a few engagements. If you're fortunate to find a willing co-author, of course, you might avoid any fee! Either way, hiring a professional writer to help you tailor and craft your book's message is a personal choice and one that should be taken seriously.

Before you do hire a freelancer, there are three important things you must do – and I do mean MUST.

1. Get references from other clients they have worked for, and contact them.
2. Get substantial samples of their writing. By "substantial," I mean a few chapters they have edited or ghostwritten, not merely one or two pages.
3. DO NOT pay *in full* upfront. Arrange for your writer to do the first third of the book. And, pay immediately after you've reviewed and approved it. Then pay after the next third of the book is written and so on.

By following my advice you will avoid the problems encountered by a friend who hired a ghostwriter and paid his twenty thousand dollar fee in advance. My friend was fully assured that he would be happy with the final book. But the book he finally received was not in his "voice," the tone was negative, and the message was far from what my friend wanted to convey. It would have required almost an entire re-write, which the writer refused to do. So, my friend lost his twenty thousand dollars and still has no book. DON'T LET THAT HAPPEN TO YOU!

Celebritize Yourself Fact:

"If time is of the essence – and it usually is – the six to twelve months it could take you to write your own book might be cut in half by a professional freelance writer who can deliver the bestseller you want."

Getting Your Book Into Print

Books are written to be read. Manuscripts are created to be published. For all the hard work that you invest in developing your message and writing your book, consumers must eventually be handed a published book. Fortunately, the process of book publishing has never been easier. But with all of the publishing options available today it can also make your decision as to the best way to get published even more difficult!

Here's the good news: new trends in publishing provide many more creative and innovative publishing choices beyond the traditional self-publishing options of only a few years ago.

In addition to the traditional publishing model, you'll find a variety of unique collaboration possibilities between authors and publishers and an unlimited number of ways you can structure a book deal. Authors now have at least four different publishing alternatives to choose from. As they can be confusing to authors new to the industry, I will briefly discuss the pros and cons of each a bit later. You can then decide which option makes the most sense for you in terms of your overall objectives for your book, budget, resources and marketing strategy.

You must also think about how to get your book into bookstores. The truth is, unless you've once traveled these roads, you won't necessarily know the challenges of getting bookstores to carry your books. It's not only a problem for would-be celebrities, it's also a problem for the rich and famous, and for those whose books are published by the big-name publishing houses.

I remember when Don Imus released his book back in the '90s. He ranted on his show about not finding his book in a local bookstore in his neighborhood. Unusual? Not really. Around the same time, Dave Barry, a well-known, nationally-syndicated columnist, had just then released his own new title and was having a similar problem – despite his huge book tour. Barry took the humorous approach and wrote a few columns about his life on a book tour in an effort to get his book into stores where they weren't otherwise to be found.

Yes, that was back in the '90s when there were also far fewer books published. Today nearly 300,000 new books are published annually – thanks largely to the new self publishing opportunities. And the competition for space on book shelves in national chain stores, national superstores, and even independently-owned bookstores is absolutely fierce.

I'm forever explaining to professionals who are authoring a book – and are confused about whether or not to self-publish – that unless you're one of the few who receive a big advance from a traditional publisher, the only other advantage in going the traditional route is a publishing company's sales and distribution capabilities.

But above and beyond retail distribution, you can promote yourself and your book online. A drive-time radio host mentions your name and the title of your book in the same sentence; both are easily searchable online when listeners get home. You and your book appear on an afternoon TV talk show; interested viewers can see your interview and order online from their laptop.

Online articles link to your book's Web site or send people directly to Amazon.com. If your book reads well, looks good, and is available from a reputable online e-tailer like Amazon.com, readers will feel comfortable buying it – hopefully in droves!

But consider this: no matter who publishes your book, the contents (what's between the covers) MUST be as good as you can make it!

Before we further discuss your publishing choices, let's define some terms because publishing, as with other industries, has its own unique language that you should understand – especially if you decide to self-publish.

1. **Publishing:** The industry concerned with the producing and disseminating of literature or information – or making information available to the public.

   Traditionally, the term refers to the distribution of printed works – such as books and newspapers. Digital information systems and the Internet expanded the scope of publishing to include electronic resources such as the electronic versions of books and periodicals, as well as Web sites, blogs and so forth. (Wikipedia.com)

2. **Publisher:** Someone engaged in publishing periodicals, books, or music. (Onelook.com)

3. **Editor:** A person responsible for the editorial aspects of publication; the person who determines the final content of a text. (Onelook.com)

4. **Literary agent:** An agent is someone who represents writers and their written works to publishers, assisting in the sale and deal negotiation. They usually earn their living by taking a part of a writer's earnings, traditionally ten to twenty percent. (Wikipedia.com)

5. **Book Distributor:** "...represents the interests and activities of book publishers. There are two primary functions of a book distributor: sales and distribution. For independent publishers, it often makes more sense to hire a distribution company. These companies not only handle all aspects of the selling process, but they have the contacts and reach to access all the major sales outlets nationwide. They also ship, bill, collect, and handle customer service. These "back-office" operations are essential to the entire selling process and are best serviced by experienced professionals steeped in the bookselling process and retail and wholesale service requirements and expectations." (***The Midpoint Handbook*** – "The 7 Keys to Publishing Success")

6. **Book Wholesaler:** "People often confuse book wholesalers and book distributors. Both are essential to a publisher's success, if not survival, but they differ greatly in the services they provide. The book wholesaler should be seen as a service provider to bookstores. They do not create demand, rather they respond to demand. They serve the interests of bookstores and other retail outlets. Their main objective is to get product A to store B in the shortest possible time and at the lowest possible cost. Two of the largest book wholesalers are Ingram and Baker and Taylor." (***The Midpoint Handbook*** – "The 7 Keys to Publishing Success")

Celebritize Yourself Fact:

"But consider this: no matter who publishes your book, the contents (what's between the covers) MUST be as good as you can make it!"

The Case for Traditional Publishing

With traditional publishing, the author is genuinely the author and the publisher is genuinely the publisher. Another identifying trait of the traditional publisher is a royalty paid to the author by the publishing house.

First, let's discuss the downside of traditional publishers. They can take 12 to 18 months to publish your book. That's a long time particularly when you're trying to rapidly build your celebrity name. But those are the facts: 12 to 18 months to bring your book to market.

But, there is also a lot to recommend about traditional publishers. For one thing, they add credibility to your book. Large publishers like Simon & Schuster, Random House, Harper Collins and a host of others are names we recognize and trust in this industry. Their name on your book indicates an investment of time, talent and money.

A traditional publisher may also pay you. With your other options, you pay. Most traditional publishers will pay an advance for your book, in addition to royalties, which are a percentage of the publisher's sales on the book. Traditional publishers also pay for editing, cover design, printing, shipping to bookstores, handling returns, promotion and so forth.

But, the choice to go with a traditional publisher is not always yours. It's difficult to land a traditional publisher. You will probably need a literary agent to represent you to acquisition editors at publishing houses. Agents know how to negotiate the best book deals and they have relationships with publishers who depend on agents to bring them good titles.

Of course, finding a literary agent to represent you can sometimes be as difficult as finding a publisher to publish your book! It's definitely a marketing challenge. Reference books in libraries list literary agents, as do Google and other search engines. Most literary agents represent specific genres of books they specialize in, so you want to prepare a customized list of these agents who deal in yours. Then send them your book proposal (which you can learn more about online). The agent will either reject you or elect to represent you.

Of course, you can pitch to publishers directly by following essentially the same procedure that you follow to solicit agents. Identify publishers who specialize in your type of book with a query letter and a book proposal directed to the acquisition editor. Then sit back and await their response. But, if you work directly with a publisher and get a book deal, get legal advice from a publishing industry attorney before signing a contract.

Whether you proceed through a literary agent or work directly with a publisher, you'll need a very aggressive marketing campaign to get the job done.

Let's say you land that traditional publisher. Don't make the big mistake that happens to most novice authors (and I'm talking about highly educated, brilliant people in their own industries). They assume that once they've got a publishing contract with the traditional publisher, their book will be well promoted. I hate to be the bearer of bad news, but nothing could be further from the truth! You see, publicity departments at major publishing houses are usually charged with getting exposure for ALL their new titles each season. But, common business sense will tell you that their major efforts have to be focused on those authors who received the biggest advances. A publisher, who invests a six- or seven-figure advance, expects the book to be a bestseller. But for that to happen, publicity efforts must be heavily supported.

Most authors get small or even no advances from traditional publishers, thus they get little to no promotion. This partly explains why publicity firms such as mine succeed in business. We become champion publicity-getters for authors who get lost in the shuffle with traditional publishers. Since you're that new author, you too must become that marketer extraordinaire – whether you go with a traditional publisher or you self-publish.

So if you are willing to wait 12 to 18 months for your book to be published, then consider traditional publishing. On the other hand, if you want a book now, if you KNOW that your book can find a solid market, and if you want that five-star marketing campaign, read on for other options that might be a better choice for you.

Celebritize Yourself Fact:

"Whether you proceed through a literary agent or work directly with a publisher, you'll need a very aggressive marketing campaign to get the job done."

The Case for Self-Publishing

With the self-publishing option you essentially choose to set up your own publishing company. You are the publisher. You use the same business model as do traditional publishers. You are responsible for everything associated with being a publisher.

The first step: find a team to support the book with ghostwriting, editing, manufacturing, publicity, distribution and so forth. This team will be invested in the project with you and have similar goals for the book's success, because their income may partly depend on its success.

Self-publishers work similarly to large publishers, but with the benefit of today's technology, you can economically replicate the traditional publisher model. You have fewer books to market so you can give your book more effort and you will have more time to market your book than would the traditional publisher who pushes their books only in the fall and spring.

Self-publishing is an attractive option if you can perform the functions of a publisher. If so, there are lots of benefits. You can get your book to market more quickly than can a traditional publisher; nobody will cast judgment on whether your book is "good enough." Plus, you won't earn a tiny percentage of the sales – or royalties – as you would with a traditional publisher. The returns for investment of your time and money in book promotion are all yours.

Another plus of self-publishing: a self-published book will only go out of print when the author wants it to. In contrast, the shelf-life of a traditionally published book can be 3 to 6 months for a book that doesn't sell well.

With each passing year, self-publishing wins more and more fans. In fact, many recent bestsellers started as self-published titles; *The One-Minute Manager, What Color is Your Parachute?* and *The Christmas Box* are only a few examples. Yours can be next!

Celebritize Yourself Fact:

"With each passing year, self-publishing wins more and more fans."

The Case for Print-on-Demand Publishing (P.O.D.)

Print-on-demand companies are professional service providers who can put your words into a reader's hands with a simple process. You pay companies, such as iUniverse.com and Xlibris.com, an upfront fee according to the specific services you want them to provide – copyright registration, copy editing, book review, and so forth. These companies provide every pre-press service necessary to produce your book. But do understand that these print-on-demand companies are not actually publishers in the traditional sense. They're more of a printing operation. It's a hybrid self-publishing model – you're the publisher, but you outsource whatever services are necessary to produce the book.

Their real advantage is that you can "feel" your way into the market. It's an economical way to test the demand and market for your book. You might later sell the book to a traditional publisher if the initial run is successful. I like to say print-on-demand is a good starter kit.

Its downside? P.O.D. companies make money by printing books. They don't sell books. So, lack of distribution is the big drawback. While P.O.D companies might help get your book into Amazon.com and make it available on their own Web site, bookstores won't carry P.O.D. titles because unsold copies are not returnable to the publisher, as are traditionally published books.

This is bad news to the many uninformed authors who might have expected otherwise.

Celebritize Yourself Fact:

"Print-on-demand companies are professional service providers who can put your words into a reader's hands with a simple process."

The Case for Joint-Venture Publishing

For the busy executive or would-be celebrity who has written a book, but has no publishing industry knowledge - nor the time or interest to get educated – there is the option of joint-venture or co-op publishing. It's another hybrid between traditional and self-publishing. Here you work with a publisher who has the team put together for you.

With self-publishing, you must organize your own team. With the joint-venture, you work with a pre-existing team who will be your publisher. You're simply the author.

The essence of the joint-venture is that you and the publisher bring different things to the table. How you divide responsibilities is negotiable. There are many variations of "deals" from publisher to publisher in joint-ventures. You might have to invest some capital and revenue share, too. Deals range anywhere from 100% profits to the author, who fully finances the production, to a 50/50 or 40/60 percent split of profits – or even lower – depending on the amount of capital you invest.

A joint-venture is a great choice if you have the finances to hire a professional team to publish and distribute your book. You can then devote your valuable time and energy to spreading the word while enjoying the rewards and benefits of being a published author and celebrity.

You can find excellent joint venture publishers on the Internet, at book conventions and written about in the publishing industry trade magazines. I've worked with many over the years, all of whom I recommend for different reasons, like Greenleaf Publishing, Book Publishers Network, Warren Publishing, Tate Publishing and Beaufort Books.

Celebritize Yourself Fact:

"For the busy executive or would-be celebrity who has written a book, but has no publishing industry knowledge - nor the time or interest to get educated – there is the option of joint-venture or co-op publishing."

Chapter 6:

From Local Celebrity to National Celebrity

"Live out of your imagination, not your history."

~ Stephen Covey

S o, now you've got your book – or you are at least on your way to having your book. What do you do next to celebritize yourself? Glad you asked! In this chapter we'll talk about how to use your book to open the door to the media and make yourself a celebrity.

That's really how you must think of your book. It's a tool. So many of us envision the words "book" or "author" and instinctively think: "millionaire!" But unless you're a top tier author who sells millions of books per year, that's simply not reality.

Most of my published clients use their book as a tool to produce many other wonderful, celebrity-fueled benefits. An additional revenue stream is secondary to them. Your book can lead to guest interviews on radio and TV, newspaper and magazine articles, speaking opportunities before local and national groups, clubs, conferences, and seminars. Yes, your own book can produce all this and more.

But all of these grand things will happen to you only if you keep your objectives straight and remember why you wrote the book – you want to become a celebrity. So, let's put into perspective the dream of immediate fame through mass media coverage, versus the reality of how your rise to celebrity is more likely to happen through a ripple effect. Media coverage usually starts locally, say within a 5- to 50-mile radius. It then expands regionally and later nationwide – if national exposure is your goal.

This "reality" should not be a dream-crusher. This reality should be a dream-*builder*. You need to correctly estimate how much work and effort will be necessary to reach celebrity status within your field. Then you can plan intelligently and not get sucker-punched by trick questions or the backstabbing wannabes who populate the territory.

More specifically, "reality" means that you start from where you are and branch outward. *How?* How do you take your dream to become a celebrity, and use your book as a tool to achieve celebrity status?

It, of course, has much to do with creating "buzz," or knowing how to capture media attention. One media follows others, so even a small article in the local town press has value. And, of course, you need to gain experience to be well prepared for the major media. Only when you expertly handle a radio interview with a local talk show host can you feel at ease on *Oprah, the Today Show* or *Good Morning America* – appearances that are every writer's dream.

In this chapter I will show you how to reinforce your decision to *Celebritize Yourself.* There are only six degrees of separation between that businessperson or self-starter who writes a book and gets mentioned in their local paper, and the one who springboards to a debate with Bill O'Reilly on prime time. This possibility is more realistic today in this age of non-stop cable chatter and instant blog celebrities.

Talk radio shows have many hours to fill. The talent pool constantly needs replenishment. You might well be that next celebrity guest. And the next. And the next. Voila...soon you, too, are a celebrity!

Celebritize Yourself Fact:

"Your book can lead to guest interviews on radio and TV, newspaper and magazine articles, speaking opportunities before local and national groups, clubs, conferences, and seminars. Yes, your own book can produce all this and more."

Big Celebrities From Small Ripples

So, think of your book as a pebble that will make that ripple. Every celebrity starts somewhere. You, too, must start *somewhere* if you are going to get *anywhere*.

Unfortunately, people miss opportunities because they wait to get started. They wait to lose weight, wait to build a bigger business, wait to save more money, to have a better address, or more free time, to get a college degree or even cosmetic surgery! Celebrity has nothing to do with where you live, your bank account, your looks, or your age.

If you're "waiting to pull it all together," guess what? It's time to end the waiting game. It's time for action. You ask, "Where do I start?" That's simple. It starts with you and *your decision to become a celebrity.*

It means deciding exactly what you want to achieve. Where is the end of the road? Envision it exactly. With that picture in mind, make it a game for yourself. But, as long as you're creating the game, make it a game that you can win.

Anticipate the obstacles you must overcome and work out how you will overcome each. For example, what must you do to write your book? That's step one. Do you have time to write? A quiet space to write? Money for a ghostwriter? You see the point.

Work out each step until you get to the end goal. Your walk on the path will take unexpected turns. But, if you stay focused on the goal, you'll know which new turns are the correct ones.

It's also important to set short and long-term goals, including realistic estimations of the time needed to accomplish each. Unrealistic targets that underestimate the effort necessary to get the job done will give you a sense of failing at the game. And, if that drags on too long – you're toast!

Or perhaps, burned toast.

So, all this requires planning. Loads of books can help you write a plan, set targets, goals, timelines, etc. The point is, you've decided to be a celebrity and that's absolutely wonderful! Now do something to really make it happen.

Right now, today is when you have the three basic ingredients to become a celebrity: 1) expertise to share, 2) the desire to be a well-known opinion leader in your field, and 3) the plan to get a book written as your tool to become a celebrity. These three ingredients must be melded and fused together as part of your life. It all starts from where you stand at this very moment. Yes, right here, right now. Believe it!

Before we move on, think about a clear blue pond. Its size or depth doesn't matter. You can change the very nature of that pond simply with the toss of a tiny pebble. That pebble creates little ripples which become bigger and wider as its energy spreads outward farther and wider. Soon the entire pond has been touched by your one small act of tossing that one pebble.

Imagine your future celebrity standing on the banks of the pond of "fame." Your book is a pebble you cast into the big wide world of media interviews and appearances, articles that quote you as an expert, book reviews, profiles in newspapers and magazines, invitations to speak at conferences and seminars, and so forth. Soon, paid speaking engagements come along. So do requests to hire you as a consultant.

The ripples will come. They will also get bigger and bigger as you become better known. But first you must make the book happen, then use it effectively to create those ripples. The good news: I will show you exactly what to do once you have your book. So test your throwing arm. Get that book ready. Let 'er ripple, now!

Celebritize Yourself Fact:

"It starts with you and your decision to become a celebrity."

Coming Soon: Your Book

For your book to become your marketing tool, you must become the architect – the carpenter, if you will – of your very own celebrity. Fame and fortune won't spring from the book itself. You get that because the book produces media interviews, entree, access, credibility, new clients, new business opportunities, speaking engagements, recognition and so forth. In sum, the book positions you as an expert in your field.

So, the book is more than just a book. It's even more than that pebble skip in a pond. The book illuminates your path. The best part is that you understand this in advance. Too often, people don't understand the power of a book until it's too late, or they finally come to me when their book is already two or three years old.

Before the stage lights flash on and the curtain arises, you have much to do to prepare for the day your book is published. This work must begin months before the book's publication.

One obvious first step is to build advance excitement for your book's arrival. Let people know it's coming. Put your friends, family, business associates and clients on notice.

Develop a Web page for your book (a "landing page"). If you already have a Web site for your business, link the book's landing page to your Web site. The publicity for your book will then also increase awareness of your business.

Your landing page must be more than beautiful. It also needs great sales copy. This landing page is a major point of sale. Attracting people to go to your landing page is only the first step. The second step is to get them to buy your book. That's why you need not only a great Web page designer, but also great sales copy that can produce great sales.

Visitors who go to your Web site are prospective readers for your book or clients for your business. Give them the incentive to sign up for a free report or e-newsletter or your blog. Yes, you might ask, "How will I find time to write a free report or a monthly newsletter if I will be so busy promoting my book?" The answer is the same as for writing your book – hire a ghostwriter!

With the book close to its release date, decide whether you will handle your own book promotion or hire a publicity firm. I'll talk more about hiring a publicity firm, but under either option, it's a good idea to start building your own list of media contacts – if you haven't started already.

List all local media: radio hosts, TV anchors, journalists at your local major daily newspaper and local magazines. Don't forget your community newspaper, which almost everyone reads to find out what's happening in their neighborhood! One quick way to get this information is to go to the particular media's Web sites; they're the easiest and most regularly updated sources of contact information.

When you have "advance" copies of your book or the final copy, notify everyone on your list. Start contacting the Community Relations Manager (CRM) at your local bookstores to line up book-signings. Most love to showcase local authors who then bring in local business (friends, relatives and business associates)!

This doesn't seem very daunting, does it? In fact, it can be great fun! The key is to remember:

1. You are no longer just a civilian. You are now an author.
2. Your book is no longer just a book. It is your marketing tool – your key to celebrity.

Celebritize Yourself Fact:

"For your book to become your marketing tool, you must become the architect – the carpenter, if you will – of your very own celebrity."

Creating Buzz: Is a Public Relations Firm for You?

Let's talk about hiring a public relations firm to make you that celebrity. Publicity is my field of expertise (which explains why I could build a bit of celebrity for myself). My firm, **Event Management**

Services (http://www.emsincorporated.com), has provided
publicity for hundreds of aspiring celebrities for nearly twenty
years. So, I certainly know something about it! Let me then share
10 important tips to help you find the right firm to help you gain
success as a celebrity:

Tip # 1:
Find a firm that specializes in your industry, particularly if you want publicity for your business (regardless of whether or not you have a book).

The public relations industry has specialists in almost every field
– real estate, aviation, religion, health, law, and so forth. Finding a
firm that specializes in your industry is an ideal start if the other
important criteria for choosing a PR firm are met.

WHY? A firm that specializes in your industry understands
that industry's particularities. They will have an understanding of
its special terms; what's significant, what's newsworthy, and what's
not. They won't waste time researching on your dollar, and they
will already have strong media relationships with journalists and
publications of interest to you.

I can share one embarrassing story, but I'm sure you'll be
forgiving. One irate gentleman told me I cost him around $150,000
because I didn't take his call from a year earlier when he was first
searching for a PR firm. He hired another firm, spent nearly
$150,000, and wound up with virtually nothing to show for it.

The problem? This PR firm knew absolutely nothing about
the natural health industry – this man's business. A cancer
survivor, he had developed a line of nutritional products for
cancer patients. The big New York PR firm he hired collected a
hefty monthly retainer for the necessary research to understand
this industry and products and develop a PR strategy to get

national media exposure. Since this firm knew nothing about his industry, they had to start at ground-zero to learn about it and then make new industry-specific media contacts.

After much time, money and promises, their final result: a paltry story published in an obscure community paper and a very expensive video news release. That's when this gentleman and I finally spoke. I learned that he had first called my firm before he hired the other firm (at that time, we specialized in the natural health industry). But since he and I never spoke directly, he chose this other firm. He was upset because he had invested a lot of money and got no results, so he partly blamed me for this mishap. He hired my firm after we spoke, but when I reviewed the other PR firm's work, it was apparent they knew nothing about his industry and its technical jargon. They didn't understand how to position the client, how to pitch his topic to the media, or to whom to pitch it.

Having said all that – and assuming that you have a book – try to find a firm that specializes in promoting books. Book promotion is an industry unto itself with its own unique needs and idiosyncrasies.

Tip # 2:
Hire a firm that specializes in the right media for you.

Not every PR firm is a master at every medium. Most PR firms specialize in print media (obtaining editorial coverage in newspapers and magazines), which is a wonderful vehicle to spread a message. But, when interviews on radio and TV are also desirable (which they must be if you are an author!), make certain that the firm has a great track record in landing broadcast media interviews for their clients, as well.

Tip # 3:
Ask for sample campaigns. It's the only way to get a feel for the work that the firm has done for other clients.

Yes, you will see their best foot forward, but the sample campaign they present to you demonstrates their skill and proficiency at obtaining media exposure.

Tip # 4:
Get names of other clients whom they've represented and contact them.

Ask the references about the firm's weaknesses and strengths. Find out how quickly their account manager responded to their needs. Would they hire the firm again? Most importantly – what results did they get?

Tip # 5:
Make sure their fees are reasonable.

Don't look for the most expensive firm. They're not always the best. A fancy address in a major city means high fees because they are in a high-rent district. This does not always make them more effective.

Tip # 6:
Try to find a firm whose fees are tied to performance.

Particularly in the book industry, you'll find PR firms who charge only for the actual media appearances they obtain for you. Other PR firms charge a monthly retainer. You pay for their "best efforts" without guarantee of media exposure.

Tip # 7:

Find a firm that understands your business and convinces you that they can get the job done.

This is important because when an account manager pitches you to the media and is turned down initially, he must sufficiently understand your topic to overcome the objections he might run into. More education about you and your message is sometimes vital.

Don't be shy about asking who will write your press releases and who will represent you to the media. How long have they been with the firm? What is their experience? Don't let your campaign be delegated to some rookie just out of college.

Tip # 8:

Don't choose a local firm when you need regional or national media exposure.

After the initial meeting, your PR firm will require little "face time" with you. So, look for the best firm – period. Don't concern yourself about where the firm is located. Our firm, for example, is in the Tampa Bay area of Florida, but our clients are nationwide.

Tip # 9:

Find a firm with enthusiasm.

PR firms are in the business of promotion; to succeed they must be interested in what you're promoting! I frequently turn away business if the topic doesn't excite me, because I know that I won't do my best job. On a personal note, I'm feverishly opposed to psychotropic drugs and once turned down a large contract from a major pharmaceutical company (to their disbelief) because I refused to promote their products.

With that viewpoint, how could I possibly promote them? So, I don't. My position is also fair to the prospective client. The firm pitching them to the media must thoroughly believe in what they do – and that's what I tell every prospect that I reject!

Tip # 10:
Hire a firm that you feel comfortable with and would enjoy working with.

If all the other criteria match, you should have no problem with this last one. If the PR firm that you hire truly supports your cause and is a real member of your "team," it can be a very rewarding experience. I've built many long-term relationships and associations with clients that go far beyond promoting their company, product, book, or service.

Celebritize Yourself Fact:

"PR firms are in the business of promotion; to succeed they must be interested in what you're promoting!"

The Extra Business Card: Think of Yourself as an Author

Congratulations! You have a new title: author. Wear this title comfortably. Yes, it can be awkward at first, I know. We so often call ourselves by more familiar titles: boss, employee, manager, consultant, CEO, entrepreneur. But those, too, are titles that we were once unfamiliar with.

Transitioning from civilian to author acts as training wheels for your new celebrity. Few authors are instant celebrities. But as I've pointed out earlier, most modern celebrities do author a book – even many books. And they do so early in their careers.

So, the sooner you become comfortable with yourself as an author, the sooner you'll feel like that true celebrity. This is a process.

Becoming an author is one of those first important steps. When I say "refer to yourself as an author," take that quite literally.

Like most things, a book undergoes a process. You dream about it, think about it, plan it, write it, edit it, rewrite it, edit it, print it and, eventually, publish it. You, as an author, evolve similarly. Before you published your book, you were just someone with an idea. Once the book was in your eager little hands, with its bright and polished cover and your byline, you officially became an author.

So, think like an author. Better yet, talk like one. For the next few days, introduce yourself as an author. Whether you are a CEO, homemaker, chef, politician or policeman, for the next several days your official title is "author."

Print business cards with your title – "Author" – beside your name. Reproduce the book cover proudly on the card. I recommend this highly.

Of course, every situation is different. In a traditional business greeting, introduce yourself as an author, but present your usual business card. In other situations, when dealing with the public or a prospective media gatekeeper, present your author business card.

More often than not, you will use your author card instead of your business card. Why? Because "author" IS your new business. That's the point; "celebrity" is not something you do in your spare time or that happens by accident. Becoming a celebrity is a full-time job.

And you've only just started!

Celebritize Yourself Fact:

"Transitioning from civilian to author acts as training wheels for your new celebrity."

Turning Books Into Big Bucks: Getting the Buzz Started

The strategy is usually to start locally and branch outward. Think about the growing ripples in our bigger pond of celebrity. I think it's important to end this chapter by using the ripple effect metaphor to reinforce how new this will feel to you. There is a difference between talking about celebrity and becoming a celebrity. This difference is the difference between a pond and an ocean.

Every celebrity has his or her own learning curve. Some learn quickly, others take time. Regardless, every future celebrity makes mistakes: a joke that falls flat during a speech, an abrasive email to an important media contact, a burned bridge from an event no-show. These little mistakes, made too often, can derail celebrity.

Even a mere matter such as ordering too little – or too many – books for a reading or signing can turn opportunity into failure. That big bookstore chain in town may not give you another event date. But how do you know how many books to ship until you've gone through this a few times?

And what better place to "shape your act," so to speak, than where you feel most comfortable – locally? Getting press coverage is also not easy. (Later, I'll give you important tips on how to get media attention.) And building media contacts takes time. One radio appearance turns into two, which turns into three – but only with persistence and diligence. Making it onto a local TV station in some major cities can be as difficult as a shot on the *Today Show*, yet there is always room for one more author – celebrity – if you handle yourself professionally, with persistence.

Take your time to intelligently make your mark. Build on your contacts. Schedule events. Appear at signings and readings – whether at the biggest chain bookstore in town or the smallest mom-and-pop used bookstore – with enthusiasm, vitality, humor, and your great message. Be prompt, be professional, be persistent.

Even the biggest towns are small when it comes to local newspapers, magazines, radio, and TV employees. These gatekeepers remember names, faces, an attitude, a gesture, a remark, or an affront. They have short attention spans and long memories. When you consistently provide trouble-free, audience-pleasing appearances time and again, the gates eventually open and something truly exciting starts: a buzz.

A buzz is something that you create. It starts small, like those pond ripples. It builds slowly. But when cultivated and capitalized on, the buzz eventually gets too loud to ignore. This is our goal when we work with you: create a buzz that makes your name, your face, your book, and your message instantly synonymous – and ultimately recognizable.

So, where does your celebrity start? Locally.

So, where does your buzz start? From within.

Celebritize Yourself Fact:

"Every celebrity has his or her own learning curve. Some learn quickly, others take time."

Chapter 7:

How to Be a Great Radio or TV Guest (and Be Quoted in the News!)

"It's the message, not the medium that is the problem. If the content is wrong, it is wrong in all of its media forms. All the gorgeous streaming video and razzle-dazzle delivery systems won't make it any better…"

~ Ellen Hume, Media Analyst and Journalist

Writing a book is only half the battle. Spreading the word about your book is where the *real* work begins. With this new job comes much-needed understanding that promoting and marketing your book will probably be quite different from anything you've ever done before.

Some people I speak with assume they will be "natural" on the air because they're public speakers or teachers. I cringe when I hear this because the same rules of professional speaking don't apply to appearing as a guest on radio and TV. It's a classic case of someone not knowing what they don't know. Yes, there are similarities between public speaking and media appearances – but there are also many differences which, overlooked, might make the difference between a successful and a failed media interview.

For example, a public speaker who stands at a podium speaking to a group of people is in a structured environment. It's a one-way communication – speaker to audience. In this forum, a speaker has perhaps 30 minutes to an hour to convey their message. Well, being interviewed by the media requires a very different skill set! As a media guest you must learn to speak in sound bites – never exceeding 90 seconds. Longer answers to the interviewer are likely to be cut off.

Most celebrities appear casual on radio or TV. And it looks easy, but it takes a lot of work and twice as much practice to truly become comfortable before the cameras, behind a microphone, or when talking to a reporter.

Even "naturals" on the air need coaching on how to weave a story, deliver a fact, or sell themselves so they remain in a viewer's consciousness long after they've turned off the radio or TV, thrown away the newspaper, or logged off of the Internet.

In this chapter, we discuss the qualities of a good guest on radio and TV, and how to give an effective print interview that will get your story published. And, of course, I'll highlight the importance of being as good as you can be when showcased in the media. Results are important to the goal of celebritizing yourself.

So, how do you become a good guest or a good interviewee?

1. **Be entertaining**
2. **Be informative**
3. **Be motivating**

Celebritize Yourself Fact:

"Most celebrities appear casual on radio or TV. And it looks easy, but it takes a lot of work and twice as much practice to truly become comfortable before the cameras, behind a microphone, or when talking to a reporter."

Interview Tip # 1:
Be Entertaining

We all love to be entertained. Even if your expertise is quantum physics, your appearances on radio and TV and even in print must be engaging, informative, educational and, in a word, *entertaining*.

No, I'm not recommending that you study theatrics or bring along props to every interview, but do your best to engage the host and your audience. Appear real, authentic, accessible and likeable. Talk to your audience as you would to your family, co-workers, and friends – and you'll increase the likelihood that your audience will actually listen closely to what you have to say.

Keep in mind that while creating your celebrity is your ultimate purpose for appearing on the air, most hosts, quite frankly, don't care about your goals. They care about achieving their own goals, building their own success and celebrity. They care about their show's ratings. That's their job security. So, when they invite you on as a guest, they expect you to engage their audience because the audience will stay tuned in. That is why your message – and how you deliver it – is so vitally important.

Every show is different, as is every audience. Some shows are serious, others are fun and snarky. Some are on morning shows, others play late at night. These factors, too, will affect your performance. But never let them affect your ability to entertain.

Be enthusiastic and positive no matter what time of day it is and no matter who you're talking to. Smile when you're on the air. Smiling gives your voice a more attractive tone.

Smile while you talk, and your voice sounds richer and happier. Listeners and viewers pick that up. Conversely, if you frown, they'll pick up on that, too. These are a few of the precious "clues" that your audience gets to form an impression of you. So, smile, talk, and put out good vibes.

Remember, the popular media won't give you anything – you must earn it. You do that by making it easy for hosts to put you on the air and, in turn, giving them (and your audience) an entertaining show. If you do, I promise they will want to put you on again and again.

One producer gave a client great advice for appearing on radio or TV: "Act like nobody's listening." It's kind of the celebrity's equivalent of telling a nervous public speaker to calm their nerves by imagining the audience in their underwear! It usually works.

This brings to mind another point: listeners or viewers may be tuned in, but are just as likely to be tuned out. Think of how you listen to the radio or watch TV. Isn't it sometimes engaging, entertaining and memorable, but at other times you hear only background noise?

Your enthusiasm will be contagious. Your excitement about your message radiates to the audience. Their excitement, in turn, propels them to learn more about you and your book, product, or service after the interview. The insightful super-salesman Zig Ziglar warns: "For every sale you miss because you're too enthusiastic, you will miss a hundred because you're not enthusiastic enough."

And be conversational with your host. If there are callers, speak to them as you would to old friends. This signals to your audience that you are friendly, approachable, and relaxed; someone they would want to work with, or take advice from.

Also be confident. It's the life-blood of success. If you're not that confident about working with the media yet, then take a page from Arsenio Hall's vast treasury of life quotes: "I don't possess a lot of self-confidence. I'm an actor, so I simply act confident every time I hit the stage." Well, there you go. Whether confidence gushes from you like a mountain spring – or you merely pretend that it does – it's one quality that will make your audience want to listen to you further and want to do business with you. Finally, the more you can put yourself at ease and be yourself, the better the odds of being a great success.

Celebritize Yourself Fact:

*"Even if your expertise is quantum physics, your appearances on radio and TV and even in print must be engaging, informative, educational and, in a word, **entertaining**."*

Interview Tip # 2:
Be Informative

Even the most entertaining guests might be seen as mere "filler" unless they actually have something to say. Jokes, quips, and congeniality are all fine, but at the end of the day, radio and TV producers look for guests who are easy on the eyes and ears, but at the same time, enlightening.

It's the difference between junk food and health food. Junk food may be fun and easy to get, but you don't always feel good after you've eaten it. Plus, it can have damaging effects to your health. On the other hand, health food may take some getting used to and it is not always easy to access. But your body can feel good for hours – even days – after a healthy meal as health food has a positive nutritional value.

The trick: make your "health food" as entertaining and appealing as everybody else's "junk food." It helps when you're engaged and intrigued by what it is you're saying. When your message is passionate, that passion usually shines through. But even passion won't carry the day if your information is old, stale, or unhelpful to the listener.

Up-to-date information is the order of the day in the media. You're the expert and you're expected to know the latest developments in your field. Why risk getting blindsided by a host, or worse, by a caller who happens to know more than you do about your own industry?

That's fatal. It's smart to just dive into the news and check out your subject's major Web sites before you go on the air. Pay attention to research studies, surveys, the latest government statistics, and industry developments.

Play the role of expert and do it convincingly. It will also help you build credibility with your audience. And leave the technical jargon at home. You may think that dropping technical terms make you sound more knowledgeable, but it doesn't. After all, you're not speaking at an industry convention. You must use words that people understand or they will tune you out. Your challenge is to be "informative" in a way the audience can understand. Use layman's terms as much as possible, and save the four-syllable words for your next Scrabble game.

Always be direct when answering a question. Yes, politicians do usually get away with evading questions, so why can't you? Well, assuming you have less to hide than politicians might, it's still never wise to tap dance around an answer. Hosts have no time for tap dancing guests. They want to keep their audience tuned in and they will shut you down if you don't help them.

Also, get local information whenever possible. If you're doing a talk show in St. Louis, go online and check out the *St. Louis Post-Dispatch* before the scheduled event. What stories tie into what you will be talking about? Do that in every city in which you "appear." You'll greatly increase the odds of keeping your audience tuned in.

Lastly, no matter how many interviews you do or producers you may befriend, make sure to involve your audience in the information you provide. Yes, it's your message, but listeners will only stay tuned if your message somehow applies to them.

Celebritize Yourself Fact:

"Jokes, quips, and congeniality are all fine, but at the end of the day, radio and TV producers look for guests who are easy on the eyes and ears, but at the same time, enlightening."

Interview Tip # 3:
Motivate With Your Message

Above all, you must be a cheerleader for your message.

A number of my clients over the years understood how to really motivate audiences. Through years of practice, they could always trigger a great response from their audience – no matter how few listeners tuned in. The big part of their formula was to "motivate." They created a sense of urgency with their message.

For example, if you're a tax advisor who resolves difficult IRS problems – the type that can cause you to lose your home or business to the IRS – then anyone tuning in who has this kind of tax problem will stay glued to your interview. If you're good, they'll probably buy whatever service you're selling on the air.

One client started his career as a nutritionist and had a successful clinic. But when he discovered how adept he was in the media, he changed his entire business model. He developed a message of "urgency," a message about "10 foods you should never eat." He sold so many books, tapes, and nutritional products that he found it far more profitable to spend his time in media interviews reaching thousands instead of counseling patients one by one.

How he became one of my clients is another interesting story. One Sunday morning I headed to the store to buy some bagels and lox, a traditional Jewish Sunday morning breakfast. My car radio was tuned to a talk station when I heard this guy talking about "10 foods you should never eat." Intrigued with the topic, I was simply happy to hear entertaining conversation while riding to the supermarket. Soon it was no longer merely entertaining conversation. I was absolutely riveted to the show and couldn't leave the car.

He convinced me that my health depended on knowing what these 10 terrible foods were. An incredibly entertaining story-teller, he was also a highly-credentialed and educated nutritionist. His message was informative and so motivating that I stay tuned in for the entire show and rushed to call his office on Monday. That's how he eventually became a client.

Notice, this nutritionist didn't just talk about the ill effects of sugar, cake, and candy. He created a nutritional urgency, one as important as any financial urgency. When he talked, he injected you with the need to know the "top 10 foods you should never eat."

Of course, you *wanted* his book and tapes to tell you WHY these foods were so bad. You also wanted his products in order to overcome the ill effects from consuming these bad foods your entire life. This compelling guest made the most of every interview. And he also made a fortune selling products from his talk radio interviews.

The lesson? Airtime can work similarly for you. End each interview with a "call to action." Mention the title of your book without sounding like an infomercial. Do your job well, and the host will promote your book for you and will even give out your Web site address or phone number to call. Most hosts understand why you're willing to invest your time to be on their show and they have no problem reciprocating by plugging your book.

So, when you're on the air, remember that your passion for your topic is the same passion that got you into this business in the first place. An entertaining, informative, and enthusiastic guest connects well with the audience. The audience can then become profitable customers or clients.

Celebritize Yourself:
"Above all, you must be a cheerleader for your message."

Building Wealth With Good Interviews

Let's face it: appearing on the air is hard work. There's the process of writing and re-writing press releases to keep your message current with the news. You have gatekeepers to overcome, producers to persuade, follow-up phone calls and emails to make (my company once calculated that an average of 17 follow-up phone calls are necessary to obtain one local TV booking), appearances to schedule into your already very busy life and, of course, sound bites to master.

In many ways, being interviewed on radio, on TV, and in print on behalf of your book can be as time-consuming and challenging as writing the book! So what's the payoff for all of this hard work and energy? Plenty! Good interviews produce:

- **More book and/or product sales:** Clients often come to me immediately after a media appearance to decry their lack of "instant" book sales. But, book sales do not always spike immediately after an appearance. More important is the cumulative weight of your presence in the modern media. The more you appear in the news, the more recognition you and your book will get. This "buzz" you hear so much about is crucial to book sales – especially with nearly 300,000 new books published annually. Competition for the public's attention is fierce. These days an author absolutely must plan a marketing strategy to make his or her book known – or there's no point writing it! Book sales are seldom immediate; it all depends on YOU and how effectively you promote your book.

  Recognize that book authorship and publishing is a business. Understand that it takes persistence and time to build, just as "celebrity" does!

- **New customers or clients for your company or service:** It's not only the income from your book that counts – it's also the new customers or clients for your product or service that are important. A book is part of your marketing strategy – a tool that enables you to become known as the expert in your field. The book is how you stand out from your competition. It's the key to media that will put you in front of your prospects. A book alone can reach one person at a time, while one media appearance or one speaking gig can reach hundreds, thousands, or perhaps millions of people.

- **New visitors to your Web site:** Make your Web site ground zero for your newfound celebrity status. Unlike a book, a Web site can be updated continuously. Unlike speaking engagements or media appearances, a Web site can be carefully planned and personally orchestrated. It can convey exactly the message you wish to send. Do it interactively, and you will draw readers back again and again.

- **Invited back on the show for still more recognition:** One big benefit of doing well on a show is pleasing the producer and host. They are always looking for quality guests who are hassle-free and can add value to their show. If they like your first appearance, they will probably ask you for a repeat appearance.

- **Becoming a resource for TV, radio, or newspaper journalists:** You can't measure the value of an appearance by its length. A few minutes of being interviewed on TV can be as valuable as a long radio interview. This is particularly true in your hometown where people begin to see you and hear your name frequently mentioned and, more importantly, hear your message. The credibility factor when the media asks for your opinion on the air is immeasurable. After all, if the media recognizes you as an expert, it is "positioning extraordinaire." Voila – you are now the expert in your field. Now *that's* celebrity!

- **Auditioning for the majors.** Eventually you'll be ready for national TV, but you must be prepared. National producers will want to see previous TV interviews, be it local or national. They won't schedule you unless they know what you look like and how you present yourself on camera. This is another reason to appear on TV in your local market.

- **Media follows the media.** Strange as it sounds, that's how it works. Think *Larry King Live.* The guests on his show usually relate to what's heading the news. It can work the same way on a less grand scale as well. For example, if you make the news in your local newspaper, you can become a candidate for local radio and TV show appearances.

Celebritize Yourself Fact:

"Book sales are seldom immediate; it all depends on YOU and how effectively you promote your book. Recognize that book authorship and publishing is a business. Understand that it takes persistence and time to build just as "celebrity" does!"

Instant Imaging Through Powerful and Memorable Sound Bites!

What's a sound bite? Unless you've spent a lot of time before a camera or microphone, it's not a term that you would normally be familiar with.

A sound bite is a short phrase or sentence that captures the essence of your message. Remember, "Houston, we've got a problem" from the great movie, *Apollo 13*? That's a sound bite! Or those famous, never to be forgotten words uttered by former President George H.W. Bush, "Read my lips; no new taxes." Both short phrases clearly captured the essence of the speaker's message. They're great examples of how you can create the essence of your message.

In today's information-driven world of talk radio, talk TV, newspapers, magazines, blogs, 'zines, and newsletters, you see that fast information is what people on the go want.

Who has the time or interest to sift through meandering comments or fuzzy dialogue to capture the essence of your message? That's why it's so important to keep your message short, clear, and concise. People do want to hear what you have to say; they simply don't have all day to figure it out.

Tune in to any drive-time radio talk show or morning guest spot on the local channels. You'll hear plenty of sound bites although the best proof can be found during prime time. Chris Matthews. Bill Maher. Keith Olbermann. Sean Hannity. Bill O'Reilly. Like them, love them, or loathe them, these are the new sound bite masters. A guest who wants a second shot on their shows must equally master the sound bite.

This by no means implies that you should sound like an auto-bot and repeat your well-rehearsed sound bite no matter what the question, controversy, debate or situation. You start with the sound bite, then tailor it to match the moment.

For instance, if your sound bite is from your new dating book for women over 50, the topic lends great weight to your drive-time ready sound bite: "It's never too late to date." Timely topic, right? Great sound bite, huh? You betcha! But not every host of every show you appear on will take you quite so seriously. A wiseacre male host may call your readers "long in the tooth" or "past their prime" just to shore up his "edgy" reputation. And, in response, you can't just repeat your sound bite verbatim. You've got to couch a response that is equally short and sweet.

Sound bites, like every other component of celebrity, work best over time. Every interview is a learning experience, a proving ground, an audition for the next interview. This doesn't mean you can treat them sloppily or show up unprepared. But give yourself a break. Actors have it easy; someone else writes their lines. Politicians do, too!

Not only must you write your own sound bites, but you must also make them up on the run. Don't worry, you'll soon get the hang of it. It just takes practice and honing your listening skills. It also takes getting used to being interviewed.

Many of my clients flub their first interviews. While they show up well-prepared, well-rested, and well-rehearsed, the moment that microphone or camera is turned on they feel as if "everything was sped up and there just wasn't enough time to listen accurately and respond intelligently."

As with everything else, practice makes perfect. With each interview the timing will slow down, words will make more sense, you will be better prepared and more open to a dialogue, rather than merely responding to a set of pat questions and answers. With time, you will more and more enjoy each interview, and see it as an opportunity to spread your powerful message.

Celebritize Yourself Fact:

"Who has the time or interest to sift through meandering comments or fuzzy dialogue to capture the essence of your message?"

Meet The Press

During my early days in this business, I became unbelievably excited about a print interview we had arranged for a client of mine who was a bestselling author, attorney, and asset protection advisor. He came to Tampa to promote his most recent book so, while in town, we had him scheduled to speak at the main library, plus we arranged two TV appearances, two talk radio interviews, and an interview with the *St. Pete Times*, our major daily newspaper. We were particularly excited about the print interview, as we were expecting a big story. The journalist loved our client's message and spent hours asking questions, taking copious notes. Why, she even brought a photographer for a photo shoot of the author with his book in hand.

After two draining hours, the journalist said she had everything she needed to write her story. She assured us it was going to be a full feature story because the information was so valuable to her readers. Well, after reading the paper each day but seeing no mention of my client – let alone a feature story – we followed up with the journalist. She told us she had written a great article from the interview with my client, but unfortunately, the Senior Editor had bumped it! She was as disappointed as we were.

Now, had I not been sitting in the room with the journalist and my client and witnessing for myself the interaction and energy between the two of them, I probably would have thought that my client had blown it in some manner. But I was as surprised as the journalist – and, thankfully, my client had enough experience with the media to understand that this is how it can go.

As a publicist responsible for getting media contacts for my clients, when it comes to a radio or TV interview, we can schedule a date and time with the host or producer. The show is as good as guaranteed. But we have far less control over what the media writes and whether it's the entire story or just a small mention. Those decisions are made in the editing room!

There have been numerous changes in the print media over the years. Radio and TV have also changed. But, even if you catch your radio streaming over the Internet, it's still essentially *you* talking and people listening. And TV is TV is TV. Whether your interview clip appears online or on television, it's still you talking and people listening.

However, the Internet has caused the print medium to change quickly and continually. Newspapers have lost circulation. Smaller magazines are cutting print versions and going Web site only. *Teen People* magazine, for example, folded its print magazine in favor of *TeenPeople.com*. *Elle Girl* did the same, shutting down its print periodical to focus on *ElleGirl.com*.

It makes sense. The Internet is instantaneous so it's difficult for print versions to keep up. Why wait until tomorrow morning when I can get my late-breaking news online, or 24-hours a day on TV? But while most local newspapers won't disappear tomorrow, there has been a definite shift in their business.

Still, there will always be a need for interviews, profiles, and feature stories – whether online or in print. That's where you come in. Much as we've talked about the importance of sound bites for radio and TV appearances, they are no less important in print.

The premise is the same: most editors and reporters are busy, as are their readers. They need entertaining, interesting, and informative material for their publications to keep their readers reading! When it comes to the business side of the media, the game is the same with print as it is with radio and TV. The larger their circulation, the more advertising dollars they can charge for ad space.

So, their challenge is to know the pulse of their readers and provide news that will keep their readers coming back day after day, month after month. And, that's where you come in. Your value to the media is that you have something to say that can interest their listeners, viewers, or readers.

But, when it comes to the print media – where you can be misquoted, edited, or deleted – you must follow my three rules for a successful interview that will increase your chances of getting "ink." As with radio and TV, your message and its delivery to the print media must also be:

1. Entertaining

2. Informative

3. Motivating

These core requirements for any successful media appearance, when executed correctly, mark you as a professional. Most importantly: keep your information fresh, timely and topical. If you continually update your repertoire and commit yourself to as many appearances as possible, the celebrity-effect will eventually snowball into something real and truly powerful.

Will you be ready for this success?

Celebritize Yourself Fact:

"Your value to the media is that you have something to say that can interest their listeners, viewers, or readers."

Reaping the Payoff

A good interview – whether on radio, TV, newspaper or magazine – can bring instantaneous success. But more often success is a gradual, but steady, growth in recognition. More and more people will know you because they heard you on the radio or TV or read about you in a newspaper or magazine. You can't get discouraged by what might seem like a snail's pace. We all want overnight results. Whether your success is immediate or slow and steady, the results will nevertheless be long-lasting. That's what's best about this entire process.

If you can get the media to pay attention, and if your message resonates with your audience, you'll double, triple, or quadruple the incoming calls, hits to your Web sites, emails, and so forth. But even after the hoopla subsides, that exposure will continue to sustain your business for a long while.

Potential clients find links in a months-old newsletter and may call you even years later. It happens. Your name will pop up again and again because of the flurry of recent Web activity and – bam! – months after one or two appearances, you will still get more calls.

The key is to offer something of value when attention is diverted your way. Make yourself and your book visible and available. Whenever a talk show host or reporter asks you about your book, mention the title and where it's available. Promote the book, not only on your Web site, but also on Amazon.com. Other Web sites are great, too, but most of us have instant purchase settings on Amazon.com and are more likely to buy the book from that familiar site versus an obscure self-publisher's too-long URL or less popular sites like Bamm.com, Books-A-Million's site.

Your Web site should also be fully functional and interactive so that first-time visitors who are curious after your media appearance or newspaper story will want to visit it again. Offer a free newsletter, free book excerpts, and a timely blog that is both entertaining and "on message." Frequently visit good Web sites that you like. Identify features to add to your own site to make it look as professional as possible. In truth, you can't afford an unprofessional Web site considering the time, effort, and money you will invest in becoming a celebrity!

Ensure that your phone numbers work and that your email addresses don't bounce. Don't forget to create enticing speaker materials for potential speaking engagements. This information will inevitably be requested.

Understand that promotion is a two-step process. Step one: get your message heard. You're on the air and in the news. People see you, hear you, read about you, and like what you have to say. They're motivated by your message and want to learn more. Accomplish this first step and you're on the way to celebrity.

Step two is: sell! Prospects call the toll-free phone number or visit your Web site. Friends, this is where the pay-off happens. If you're not prepared, it's all for naught. I have seen too many of my own clients (and others) not understand the importance of what's called the "back-end." And, they never make money!

Let's start with your toll-free number. Whoever answers your phones needs a phone pitch or patter that's well scripted and designed to keep the caller interested in buying. You need someone who knows how to close the sale! Whether your own staff or a call center handles the leads – the process is the same. Your phone pitch must close and you must test it to make sure it does!

More about your Web site. Unless you have a local brick and mortar business, your Web site is where you will get most of your sales – the sale of YOU, your book, your business, your celebrity! Since no sales person actually talks to your prospects, you have no mechanism to overcome objections and close the deal. It becomes even more important then that your home page be so strong it can make the sale *for* you!

I'm always amazed at how many otherwise sophisticated business people are unaware that there are "sales copywriters." It's rightfully a high-paying profession for those master copywriters who produce results. You've seen their work, but may not have realized it. For instance, those lengthy but compelling fundraising letters you get in the mail come from the huge "Direct Mail Marketing" industry. This material is written by professionals who specialize in writing copy that sells! That's why it's called "sales copy."

Back to your Web site. If this is your point of sale, then you need great copy that can close the deal! Just as you wouldn't go to court without an attorney to represent you or fly in a plane without a pilot, if you invest in a Web site, then hire a designer for the design of it, but it's a MUST to hire a sales copy writer to write the copy.

Your Web designer is a professional at designing Web sites. Unfortunately, too few collaborate with a professional sales copy writer, and few Web designers have the expertise to write good copy. A beautiful, aesthetic, functional Web creation means nothing if it can't sell. So, if your Web designer is also a professional sales copywriter (and some are) then you've struck gold!

Reap your payoff. Understand the entire selling process and you will be correctly prepared. You can succeed on that first step – creating a demand for your product or service – but without that second step soundly in place, you may not make the sale. And then you've failed.

In short, know your endgame before you begin and be fully prepared before your launch. It's the surest way to celebrity.

Celebritize Yourself Fact:

"If you can get the media to pay attention, and if your message resonates with your audience, you'll double, triple, or quadruple the incoming calls, hits to your Web sites, emails, and so forth. But even after the hoopla subsides, that exposure will continue to sustain your business for a long while."

Chapter 8:
The Celebritize Yourself Quiz

"If you can conceive it and believe it, you can achieve it."

~ Reverend Jesse Jackson

We've talked a lot about you.

We've talked a lot about celebrity.

Now it's time to combine the two and talk about how YOU fit into this CELEBRITY equation.

Anyone can finagle a radio guest spot or two – maybe some TV appearances and even a cover story. But the celebrity whose message resonates with an audience will be around for a long time.

Do you have what it takes? Have you fully assessed your reasons for celebrity? Are they valid and sincere? Can you handle the potential rejection and frustration that can come from seeking celebrity?

I do know this much – we're about to find out! I've done enough of the heavy lifting up to this point, so in this chapter let's do something different: I invite *you* to do some work!

Don't worry. There is no heavy lifting. You need not even roll up your sleeves. However, I do want you to blow the dust off your earlier, preconceived notions of celebrity and think about how you will approach the idea of more name recognition – and more business – when you achieve celebrity status.

Speaking of plans, that's why I prepared this quiz. Each of the following ten questions will help you narrow in on your own unique, specific, and self-driven purpose for attaining celebrity and it will help you to create a foolproof plan.

Celebritize Yourself Fact:

"Anyone can finagle a radio guest spot or two – maybe some TV appearances and even a cover story. But the celebrity whose message resonates with an audience will be around for a long time."

Question # 1:
What's Your Vision for Celebrity?

Before you can even finalize a plan, you must decide where you want that plan to take you. Otherwise, it's like getting on a bus without knowing your destination.

Ask yourself, "What's my vision? Where and how do I see myself?"

For one moment, I want you to dare to envision your dream – what you truly want to accomplish. No restrictions allowed. We all fantasize our dreams, but as fast as you create the vision of what will make your heart sing, you usually find a reason why you can't achieve it. That, is not allowed here!

You see, that's the trick. "Dreamers" who make good on their goals have one thing in common: a clear vision of what they want and, more importantly, a belief that they can achieve it.

Madonna once admitted, "I realize that I don't have limits. Limits are always influences that come from outside, from people who don't believe in themselves and their abilities. I firmly believe in myself. I know I can do whatever I want and that I'll always reach my goals."

Let's return to your vision or dream, with Reverend Jackson's quote in mind, "If you can conceive it and believe it, you can achieve it." So, what does your vision look like? No, I don't simply mean mere name recognition, or a whopping checking account, but the day-to-day vision of what you will be and do as a celebrity.

Let's name it. Are you a famous talk show host? A best-selling author? Is your vision more philanthropic? Perhaps you've decided to take responsibility for all of the homeless families in your community or to ensure that everyone's medical needs are met in third-world countries. Or, you've decided to become a local celebrity as a start – the real estate agent who everyone goes to when they want to sell their home. Or the hairdresser whose clients must book two to three months in advance. Whether your visions are big or small, envision yourself in that role. You'll soon find yourself becoming the very person whom you created.

So, what's your dream NOW?

Celebritize Yourself Fact:

"Before you can even finalize a plan, you must decide where you want that plan to take you."

Question # 2:
What Is Your Commitment To Your Vision?

We're talking about determination here. How far are you willing to go to make yourself a celebrity?

Thomas Edison observed, "Sticking to it is the genius! Any other bright-minded fellow can accomplish just as much as I did if he will stick like hell and remember nothing that's any good works by itself. You've got to make the damn thing work."

As we've seen thus far, building your name and getting press coverage is no easy feat. It takes know-how, talent, drive, creativity, opinions and entertainment. Above all, it takes a driving passion, a belief in yourself, and the determination to persevere.

The path to celebrity is strewn with closed doors, unanswered phones, lackluster receptions, and heavily-sighed skepticism. To land one radio interview you may have to call one, two, or even three dozen stations to find one producer who appreciates your message. For every newspaper story you land, you may have to invest weeks or months to contact the right person at the right time to pitch the right story on the right day.

There really isn't any simplistic formula that can get you there in a day or a month or two. I wish I could say otherwise. The road to success is simply a matter of (a) knowing where you want to go, (b) believing that you will get there, (c) having a solid, realistic plan, (d) not letting others pull you off your plan, (e) not allowing yourself to deviate from your plan, (f) having the discipline to work on it continuously, and most importantly, (g) NEVER GIVING UP!

Yes, there will be obstacles to overcome as you step onto the playing field. And the longer you are in the game, the more new challenges will arise that you would never have anticipated when you first began. But you're a player now. You must be willing to stick with it and play the game to win, despite any and all odds. As long as you keep your eye on that mountain top, you'll eventually arrive at "destination celebrity"!

Celebritize Yourself Fact:

"Building your name and getting press coverage is no easy feat. It takes know-how, talent, drive, creativity, opinions, and entertainment. Above all, it takes a driving passion, a belief in yourself, and the determination to persevere."

Question # 3:
What Is Your Own Unique Message?

Before you move one step closer to celebrity, you must zero in on that all-important message. I know, I've hammered that point into the ground, dug it back up, and nailed it back down again. But there's a method to this madness: for anyone to listen to you, you must have something to say that will be of value to them, and will excite you at the same time. That's why your message is all-important to your audience and all-encompassing to you.

Defining your message isn't always easy. Nor is it always obvious. But it's important to identify, because your message is what will define you. We each have a unique message and, I promise, you'll know it when you find yours.

The components are obvious: your education, your knowledge, your expertise and experience from working in your particular field. But what's *not* so obvious is that one intangible thing you're most passionate about, the one thing that relates to all of this education, knowledge and experience.

What part of it all do you enjoy most? What keeps you reading and researching to learn more? What energizes you throughout the day then motivates you to get up in the morning? That intangible we're talking about is the essence of you. It is what makes you unique. Identify it and you've got your message!

Here's an example. I've represented a number of different cardiologists over the years who have all written books. But, each had a unique message. Earlier I told you about a famous cardiologist client who wrote a book about natural health lifestyles that prevent heart problems. His book contained low-cholesterol recipes, stress-reduction exercises, and easily-understood explanations of why certain foods or behaviors can jeopardize the health of your heart. He also had his own radio show where he espoused these very things week after week.

Another cardiologist client's book was about end-of-life issues with a way to execute important life and death decisions before being afflicted with a serious health problem that would impair your ability to make decisions for yourself. His unique message stemmed from his knowledge, education and experience with patients, but the real motivation behind his passion was his own firsthand experience with a life-threatening illness. He also founded a non-profit organization that distributed affordable legal documents for people that would protect them when they could not make life and death decisions for themselves.

A third cardiologist client's book was about how to best take care of your heart. Its focus is a specific test to detect heart disease without an IV, injected drugs or substances. His personal passion was to educate people and raise their awareness about this simple test to get any heart problems properly diagnosed and treated early.

So you see, here are three cardiologists with similar knowledge, education, and experience, but each with a different focus. And since I personally know these three doctors, I can tell you that each is equally passionate about his own unique message.

Now, what's *your* message exactly? Be precise! Can you effectively communicate it to yourself? Do your friends, family, colleagues, coaches, mentors, and peers understand it? How would you clearly word it to millions of listeners, viewers, or readers?

Only when you know your message inside out can you enthusiastically leap out of bed each morning to spread it far and wide. Only then will you know that your message is ready to stand up to that last remaining obstacle – a live audience of prospects waiting for what it is that you have to sell!

Celebritize Yourself Fact:
"Your message is what will define you."

Question # 4:
Why Does Your Message Appeal to You?

I ask this question of most of my clients. Most say their message excites them because they're doing what they love to do. Biographies of successful people have this same common thread: they know what makes them most happy and they have the courage and persistence to act on it.

Alan Alda comments, "Love your work. If you always put your heart into everything you do, you really can't lose." Carly Fiorina, former Chairman and CEO of Hewlett Packard, is on record as saying, "Make the choice to do something because it engages your heart as well as your mind. Make the choice because it engages all of you."

Matt Groening, creator of *The Simpsons*, is a perfect demonstration of Fiorina's point. He said, "I thought I was going to make crazy cartoons for the rest of my life. I didn't think I'd ever get paid for it, didn't think I drew well enough, but I knew it made me happy."

Apply the same principle to your message. It must "...engage your heart as well as your mind." Your message is everything. To you. To your readers. To your audience. When it's right, it will excite and inspire you. It will have you so jazzed that you leap out of bed in the morning racing to spread your message.

You may even find yourself doing what you never thought possible.

To this day, I'll never forget the moment in my life when I hit on a cause that "...engaged my heart as well as my mind." (I love that concept.) And, it completely inspired and excited me. Yes, it was so strong, I literally leaped out of bed in the morning, excited about what I needed to accomplish each day.

That moment happened when I learned that a friend was raising money to establish a home in Thailand for the so-called "throw-away" children who lived on the streets, hustling to survive. I badly wanted to help, but couldn't drop my life, my family and my work to move to Thailand. After some introspection, I realized that it was abandoned children, in general that pulled at my heartstrings – they did not have to be in Thailand. I quickly researched the problem of abandoned children in my own community and found there were thousands of foster children who had been abused, abandoned, or neglected.

This revelation happened right before Christmas. While doing my research, I also found that foster children in my community usually went without a Christmas party of their own and had to "crash" the party of the kids in the next county.

When I heard that, I immediately and boldly told the head of the Foster Parent's Association not to worry; I would arrange a party for the county's foster children. As soon as I hung up the phone, I thought, "Oh boy, what did I just do? How on earth will I pull this off?"

Being the cautious type and never one to commit to more than I could deliver, I was shocked that those words about sponsoring the party came from my own mouth! I had only moved to the city the month before, had a new job, and no network of friends in town! Yet I had just invited more than 300 children and parents to a party I would sponsor, having no idea where or how this would happen.

What did matter was that I was committed. Yes, I was scared. But underneath it all, I was excited about what this would mean to the kids. Instinctively I knew that somehow I could make it happen.

What motivated me? A strong desire to do something special for these kids who I knew had seen more trauma in their short lives than most people will ever see in a lifetime. I was "driven" to make the event a reality. After I overcame a large and wide range of obstacles – I won't bore you with the details – 250 foster children and about 100 foster parents had a grand time. Each child left with an armful of gifts and great memories.

This fabulous success was overwhelmingly appreciated by the children and parents alike. My excitement and enthusiasm gave these children a special night – one that brought an entire community together. That was in 1989. Every year since we've celebrated Christmas with a party for foster families in my county that just keeps getting better and better.

Once I realized how important it was to me to raise awareness for the plight of foster children, I founded a non-profit organization, Cherish the Children Foundation. We work with foster children, underprivileged children, and more recently, at-risk teens. So, remember, it's the excitement and enthusiasm of your message that will drive your machine.

That's my story. What's yours? What is it about your message that appeals to you so much? Why are you so jazzed? Forget others for now. (We'll get to them in our next question.) Right now, focus on YOU. Then, focus on your message.

Write it down. Print it. Post it. Revise it. Analyze it. Poke it. Prod it. Question it. Stretch it. If it's sound, it'll bounce back and still look just as good. But if you don't ask yourself these critical questions – if you don't push and prod and pull and practice – you'll always second guess your message – and yourself.

Celebritize Yourself Fact:

"Biographies of successful people have this same common thread: they know what makes them most happy and they have the courage and persistence to act on it."

Question # 5:
Why Will Your Message Appeal to Others?

At first blush, the answer to this question may seem obvious. But it's time for a little introspection before we move on. You have your message well-defined and it appeals to you. You love it. But (here's the true test) will it appeal to others?

It's pointless to embark on this journey unless your message not only makes YOUR heart sing, but can resonate enough with others to make it all worthwhile. Otherwise you'll only be talking to yourself! Considering the hard work involved, the frustration you'll encounter, the push-through, perseverance and courage you'll need at times to continue – the reward in large part must also include the thought that you are helping others. I'm reminded of something Gary LeVox, lead singer of Rascal Flatts said, "There is no greater gift than knowing you have touched people's lives, if just for a moment."

My friends, your message has everything and all to do with its value. Its worth to others. Lots and lots and lots of others. If it has value to others, it will have value to you – spiritually, emotionally and monetarily. Otherwise, it will likely wither quietly and quickly on the vine, after it drains much of your time and effort.

This message is reinforced by a certain gentleman who came to me with his manuscript. This highly successful, affluent professional wrote a book about his spiritual awakening. As with many other authors I meet, he considered his book to be brilliant. He wanted to invest great deals of money to have it published and to have my firm promote it. After reading the manuscript, I was at a loss for words. It was more than poor writing style or grammar. That could be edited. More importantly – the words had no real message, no heart!

The book would sell to no one other than the author's closest friends, business associates, and family who might buy it from a sense of obligation. But, it was an uninspiring book. It had no life of its own! I tactfully explained this to him and referred him to a publisher friend, who also read the book and discouraged its publication.

My three cardiologist clients exemplify authors with a message that appeals to others. All three had thriving practices and each could have easily written generally about their experiences with patients. I'm certain it would have made for an interesting read. Instead, each had a message they were passionate about, a message that also served to help others. And these doctors wanted to share their important message. That passion is indeed the formula for success – right there in a nutshell.

While celebrity starts with you, it can't happen in a vacuum. It must ride on the coattails of a strong message!

Celebritize Yourself Fact:

"Your message has everything and all to do with its value. Its worth to others. Lots and lots and lots of others. If it has value to others, it will have value to you – spiritually, emotionally and monetarily."

Question # 6:
Who's Your Target Audience

It's time for another all-important question: who will benefit from your message? Why is this important? Because identifying your audience is the foundation for your entire plan: your marketing strategy for celebrity.

When you write your book, who are you writing for? When you speak to a group, who is your audience? When you pitch the media, what specific group do you most want to reach?

The pursuit of celebrity demands some marketing savvy. You must at least know some basic Marketing 101 principles, such as "define your target audience." The best sales copy for a brochure or a letter – when mailed to an audience with no interest in the message – will fall flat. Of course, it's also true that you can have the right audience, but draw no response due to a poorly written pitch or promotion piece.

My three cardiologist clients illustrate this. The first cardiologist wrote about diets and recipes, exercise and vitamin regimes. It had a broad market. So did the books of the other two doctors. But this particular theme also had a well-identified niche market – the natural health consumer.

So, his marketing strategy included speaking at health food stores and natural health conventions. Our media pitch included the general format shows, but targeted natural health radio and TV shows. In pitching print publications, we targeted not only health reporters, but also lifestyle and food editors who could take different angles from his book for different consumer groups to whom it would appeal. Crafting the message to niche audiences is smart marketing.

Every message is unique, as are audiences. Another client, whose military-related book was published by a top University Press, admitted that when his publisher asked about his book's audience, he gave the obvious answers – historians, military buffs, sociologists, and so forth. But he found after his book was published that the bigger "stealth audience" were wives and mothers whose husbands and sons had been killed in military action. Of course, that was a very different audience than what was originally envisioned. That gave us a new angle – and a new media category – to pitch. It also gave this author a brand new market to cultivate for speaking engagements, book-signings, and other promotions.

Finding the best audience for your message is essential to defining your message. It's part of the entire package. Once accomplished, you can move smoothly onto your next step – the plan for celebrity.

Celebritize Yourself Fact:

"…identifying your audience is the foundation for your entire plan: your marketing strategy for celebrity."

Question # 7:
What's Your Plan for Celebrity?

Behind every celebrity is a plan. This isn't anything new. The famous artist Pablo Picasso knew this instinctively when he advised, "Our goals can only be reached through a vehicle of a plan, in which we must fervently believe and upon which we must vigorously act. There is no other route to success."

Whether on paper or on a computer, your unique, obtainable plan starts with a defined goal and a list of specific steps that are necessary to achieve it. A well thought out action plan isn't a mere formality; it is the celebrity's lifeline to success.

There are many good references on how to create a marketing plan, so I won't bore you with that information here. But, even if you just prepare a to-do list and put it in sequential order, you'll have a great start. The first important steps are completed – you've defined your message and identified your audience. Now it's time to figure out the specific steps that are necessary to make it all happen.

Do you need a ghostwriter or will you write the book yourself? Either way, be sure your plan takes into consideration finding the time to write and/or edit. If you will write it yourself, do you need extra personnel to cover your workload if you're a business owner? Or do you need a leave of absence from work if you're an employee? Your plan also has to allow for research steps to help you decide whether to self-publish, do a joint-venture with a reputable publisher, or go the traditional route.

Okay, let's assume that your book is complete. Now what are your marketing steps? Please, *please* don't forget to include a budget for promotion and advertising. It will take some money to execute your plan.

I never cease to be amazed by how many authors contact me about how to promote their book – without any budget. If the only answer is to do it yourself, even *that* takes time and money – not to mention know-how!

To become a celebrity requires financing, make no mistake, whether you hire a ghostwriter, editor, cover-designer, printer, etc. Even with traditional publishing, you must consider the promotional costs you will have to incur post publishing.

And the best plan is next to worthless if it doesn't take into account the projected costs related to its execution. Someone must pay for postage, advertising, purchase of media lists (if you handle your own publicity), or hire a PR firm.

These money issues don't just work themselves out, so be smart. Be prepared. This question is designed to reinforce the idea that a plan is essential, as is keeping your eye on your goal.

Arnold Schwarzenegger had a great comment: "You should always have (your goal) in front of you, because at every move you make throughout the day, you can ask yourself, 'Will this get me to my goal, or will it deviate from the plan?'"

I couldn't agree with Arnold more. Even if your Celebrity is just around the corner, it's going to take more than a great message and a smooth radio voice to make it happen.

Celebritize Yourself Fact:

"A well thought out action plan isn't a mere formality; it is the celebrity's lifeline to success."

Question # 8:
When Will You Start?

> *"The most difficult thing is the decision to act;*
> *the rest is merely tenacity..."*
> **~ Amelia Earhart, Aviator**

I assume by now you've decided to move ahead. You're enthusiastic. You have a clear vision of where you want to go. You have a plan about how you will get there. Maybe your entire plan isn't in place; maybe you only have the first few steps resolved. That's good enough to start. The question then becomes, "When will you start?"

I ask this because I know how difficult it is to *start* things. I've seen it with my many clients. I've seen it in myself.

I know about all the things you need to do first; the things that absolutely must be in place before you start. But, because I've been there myself, I know all too well that if you don't just *start*, then it's time to examine what's really stopping you. Is it really all "those things," or are you holding yourself back?

If it's the latter, my recommendation is two words: baby steps. Maybe the first action in your plan is too overwhelming. If so, break down the necessary actions into their own little steps. I can assure you, once you start, your energy will re-fuel itself so that more and more energy will be created, and achieving your goals will soon take on a life of its own. I'm sure you've experienced this phenomenon in other areas of your life. The idea is to get out on the playing field somehow, someway. Let's face it: a plan is only great if it gets executed.

So, if you decided to go for celebrity - if you envisioned where you want to be and what you want to have as a result, if you got excited about it and it energizes you – then the worst thing you can do to yourself is to abandon your dream. And let's be honest – if it doesn't happen, you have nobody to blame but yourself. It's your goal, your future, your life. No matter what your religion or life philosophy, the truth is that we are each "the captain of our own ship."

So, don't disappoint yourself. Your start date may need to change, unpredictable events may temporarily hold you back, seemingly insurmountable obstacles may arise, but if you believe in yourself, and believe that you can realize your dream of celebrity, then stay on course. Be tenacious. Don't give up!

It all starts with that all-important first step.

Celebritize Yourself Fact:
"A plan is only great if it gets executed."

Question # 9:
Have You Picked the Right Teammates?

Winning at this game is never a solo activity. It takes a team effort. Who you choose to join your team will be critical to your success. So, be selective. Beware the dream-killers who pretend to be dream-makers. Choose teammates who sincerely want you to succeed; people who believe in you with the same fervor that you believe in yourself; people who can help in different ways; who can counsel you on those important decisions; who will lend their expertise in territories unfamiliar to you; who will be your coaches and cheerleaders and who will do what is necessary to get you to your end goal.

Who are these people? You may find them in the most obvious – or non-obvious – places. Perhaps it's your spouse or life partner, son or daughter, mother or father. It might be a business partner or associate, your accountant, attorney, neighbor, or Internet friend. It might even be one of your own clients. You'll spot them when you utter those first words, "I'm writing a book." You'll know them by their sincere interest in your dream, their words of encouragement, and the way they acknowledge your smart decision. It may be the services they offer or the much needed sources to which they introduce you.

Embrace them, whoever they are. Listen to what they have to say – even if they disagree with your viewpoint or seem to bring ants to your picnic. Sometimes we get so close to our dreams that we lose our objectivity. Concerned friends, family, and colleagues often bring a much-needed and objective opinion to the fray. If they're a true team member, they'll have your best interests at heart. And sometimes they may need to smooth your path.

Good teammates will prove invaluable as you tread the unknown waters of media gatekeepers with their penchant to slam doors. And, when critics knock you down, those teammates will tell you, "Look, on the playing field you're going to get knocked down and dirty once in awhile." At the same time, they'll remind you that you are a player and as long as you stay in the game – just keep swinging away at it – you have a good chance to win.

So, listen to their words of guidance. You may not always agree, but it's good to have friends who will tell you things you may not want to hear, or suggest alternate courses to the route you've chosen, or simply bolster your confidence when you need it.

It happened to me. I was amazed at the positive reaction I got when I told my friends and family, "I'm writing a book." Their support was immediate; their advice was never ending. I made many new friends and associates along the way. I built a great team and so will you. Believe it or not, it's one of the most heart-warming parts of your celebrity journey.

Celebritize Yourself Fact:

"Who you choose to join your team will be critical to your success. So be selective. Beware the dream-killers who pretend to be dream-makers."

Question # 10:
How Will You Measure Success?

We are nearly at the end of our quiz. Still this final question to ponder is possibly the most important. Why? Because when you consider your investment in valuable time, intense effort, hard-earned money, and most of all, your own commitment, you must also ask, "What's my ROI (Return On Investment)?" What's your measure of success? It might be the challenge of staying on a chartered course and overcoming obstacles – or you may want to touch the lives of others. Maybe it's simply fulfilling a personal passion. Perhaps it's to make big money!

My point: ask yourself really what you want to have at the end of the rainbow (not that there really is an "end"). But be realistic – even if you achieve your initial goals, you will periodically need new goals and new futures if you want to progress in the game. Without fresh goals, you're off the playing field. Would that make sense after all your hard work to get there?

So, before we go further, really take the time to reflect on that question, "How will I measure my success?" The answer will help you decide whether you have the passion to sustain you, whether or not the goal of celebrity truly does "...engage your heart and your mind." If you answer "yes," well done. Let's get started.

It's also okay if you answer "no." A "no" answer simply means you need to re-think your vision of what's really important to you when all is said and done.

And only *you* know the answer to that.

I'm glad that you're reading my book and have gotten this far – even if it helps you discover that you're on the wrong course. Sometimes we must try different things to find what really fits us. The challenge is to not surrender to a "comfortable" life devoid of spirit. If you keep seeking, eventually you'll find your right path, one that captures your imagination and energizes you in a way you've never felt before.

For some reason (inexplicable to me because I hate watching anyone or anything get hurt), I confess that I enjoy professional championship boxing. One of my biggest heroes in and outside of the ring is Muhammad Ali. But there's another fighter whom I also admire greatly for what he's achieved in life, especially considering his humble beginnings. George Foreman is that other great boxer. He cautions us not to compare ourselves with others, thinking she's more talented or he's smarter. Something else he said about success really rang true to me: success is really what's in your mind, it's about your spirit.

Celebritize Yourself Fact:

"The challenge is to not surrender to a 'comfortable' life devoid of spirit. If you keep seeking, eventually you'll find your right path, one that captures your imagination and energizes you in a way you've never felt before."

Bonus Question # 11:
How Did You Score?

A high score will not necessarily mean you will be a celebrity, and for that matter, a low score will not reduce your odds to become a celebrity. This is not a pass or fail quiz; it's only a chance to get to know yourself better and tie together some questions we've been raising throughout this book.

This is an open-ended quiz. Bookmark those questions that you can't answer quite yet – or didn't fully answer – and return to them later. Even those questions you answered with confidence may change with time.

First, let's talk about your message. This vital part of remaining a celebrity will continually need updating as you get more well-known on the speaking circuit and in the media. When you deal one-on-one with hundreds or thousands of individuals, you may find that their questions require you to refine, update, upgrade, and polish your message to improve its effectiveness.

So this is a quiz, but not a quiz; a test, but not a test. The process of becoming a celebrity is a never-ending journey of self-discovery through continuous growth and change.

Celebritize Yourself Fact:

"A high score will not necessarily mean you will be a celebrity, and for that matter, a low score will not reduce your odds to become a celebrity."

Chapter 9:

Find *Your* Media Niche

"Whoever controls the media – the images – controls the culture."

~ Allen Ginsberg

One objective of this book is to get you to know yourself better before you present yourself to the world. As we have seen, that can take time.

We each have different personalities. Some drive left instead of right, here instead of there. We each have different comfort zones, not only zones that differ from each other, but constantly changing relative to where we are in our lives. When we are at our best, we talk more freely, entertain more easily, our message flows more smoothly, and we're willing to share more and more of ourselves in our effort to inspire and to motivate.

But to get to our most comfortable zone, we must first be willing to leave our present comfort zone. We're adults, after all. In the real world, we must occasionally do things that make us uncomfortable. For many, the thought of "selling" ourselves gives us goose bumps. But sell ourselves we must. If we've got to get out there and create that all-important media buzz, it's best to start where we feel most comfortable – and where our message will be most readily accepted.

This does not suggest that you should target one form of media – radio, TV, or print – and focus your energies solely in that one direction. The world is too multi-dimensional for that approach. There will always be a mix of media contenders for every celebrity campaign. But my goal here is to help you familiarize yourself with it all so that you better understand the media market, and find the media that is best for you.

Of course, some people would never feel comfortable before a TV camera, but they might enjoy the opportunity to get behind a microphone. They're a perfect fit for talk radio. Others with no tolerance for live broadcast radio and TV might be far more comfortable interviewing for newspapers and magazines.

Each medium has its own pros and cons. For instance, one big advantage of talk radio is that there's a place for virtually any topic. Radio requires no travel (all interviews are done by phone from your home or office), and radio keeps us less exposed than on television. Still, radio isn't ideal for every celebrity.

Suppose that you're an interior designer, or professional photographer, or you want to feature a new line of clothes or jewelry; radio would be a less desirable medium because it's not visual. You can jump, shout, and scream about your product on the air but who will see it? TV and print would be the far better choice since you can demonstrate your products or use photos to sell your story.

So before you begin your media strategy, look at your message and your comfort zone, then ask yourself a few more questions: Is my message newsworthy? Is it consumer-oriented? Targeted to businesses? Does it have a local twist? Are there visuals to my story? What age demographic am I targeting? Am I willing to travel for TV interviews? Am I more comfortable being interviewed by phone from my home or office? The answers to these questions will help you determine which media outlets are your best fit – at least as a beginner celebrity!

Celebritize Yourself Fact:

"If we've got to get out there and create that all-important media buzz, it's best to start where we feel most comfortable – and where our message will be most readily accepted."

Getting Your Message Across on Talk Radio

Talk radio interviews are conducted by phone (with rare exceptions), so it's often the best choice for the busy celebrity. You can easily integrate interviews into your busy workday while hardly missing a beat.

Radio appearances are also generally longer than TV interviews and they require no visual props or photos. If you can discuss your topic for 20 minutes or longer, then radio is a great fit for just about any message. On talk radio, you have a conversation with the listeners, so you must be well-versed on your topic and able to handle whatever questions come your way.

A seasoned celebrity will use this air-time to effectively deliver his or her message. You must skillfully control the interview without taking anything away from the host as you deftly direct people to your Web site. The celebrity can talk about his or her product or service without sounding like an infomercial.

The format and topics of talk radio shows (mostly found on the AM dial) will vary from morning to night. Morning shows have shorter interviews during their audience's morning drive. Morning talk show hosts do not have the time for the 30-minute interview because their shows are jam-packed with news, weather, and traffic updates.

As many people listen to talk shows at work, on their computers or a radio, you'll find the mid-day shows to be business-oriented. They generally try to attract a wider range of listeners.

Evening shows have a mixed audience who mostly listen from home. And don't discount overnight interviews. While you may think that no one listens to the radio at 3:00 AM, think again. Overnight talk shows (midnight to 5:00 AM) are wildly popular with truckers, people who work graveyard shifts, public service employees, and others in 24-hour industries.

There is a lot happening with radio and it can give you a big payoff if this is your comfort zone. Sirius is still a relative infant in the mass media market, but with names like Howard Stern and Oprah, clearly the signs are "Go" for success.

Meanwhile, terrestrial radio (AM and FM stations) continues to break new ground in drive-time programming as the demand for sophisticated, intelligent, on-air talent continues to drive ongoing demand. The latest trend in programming – on both satellite and terrestrial radio – is toward female audiences, which, of course, makes total sense since 80% of all consumer goods are purchased by women.

So, the war emerging between satellite and AM and FM channels is good for everybody, particularly new celebrities. Stay apprised of these opportunities. You can use them to your advantage.

If you doubt that you can roll with obnoxious DJs or snooty talk show hosts or the listeners who call in with questions ranging from intelligent to downright unintelligible, don't worry. I will give you some great tips later to help you in your new role as a celebrity.

Celebritize Yourself Fact:

"Talk radio interviews are conducted by phone (with rare exceptions), so it's often the best choice for the busy celebrity. You can easily integrate interviews into your busy workday while hardly missing a beat."

Yes, You Can Get on TV

Television – whether local or national – is a great way to make giant strides in your ongoing quest for celebrity. TV creates trends. It can also lend huge credibility to you, or your book, product, or service.

Remember, people relate celebrities to TV. That is where so many of us get our news, trends, fads, book reviews, gossip, human interest stories, and more. By merely appearing on TV, you immediately exude celebrity credibility.

But do remember that TV newscasts communicate to their audience visually as well as conversationally. Producers look for newsworthy topics that are visual and entertaining, or informative "how-to" segments. They want compelling conversation and visuals to grab their viewer's attention. They don't want a "talking head" rattling off statistics or blatantly plugging their new book.

One trick in developing your compelling "visual" is to ask how you would explain your message to a child. What pictures would best translate it into graphics for a TV story? Here's an example: one client who owned a successful life insurance agency wanted us to arrange local and national TV appearances. Our pitch: Why life insurance is absolutely vital for women to protect themselves and their children against the death of their spouse.

Sound like something to put you to sleep? Not so! We offered far more than just the interview. We had our client show up with graphs and bullet points – short informational snippets to show the mortality rate of women versus men. The TV stations helped with the graphics and, voila, we had a very powerful visual story that was successful for both our client and the TV show. Needless to say, he sold a lot of insurance!

Also keep in mind that the morning, noon, and evening newscasts are each geared toward different audiences. Early morning shows are watched by working adults and families preparing for school. And have you noticed how the news formats shift into more of a talk and lifestyle segment sprinkled with news "updates" after 9:00 AM, when most commuters have already left for work?

Of course, one disadvantage with TV is that it requires travel, particularly if you're looking to be a celebrity beyond your local market. Also, you'll find some cities have NO TV shows with a format for guests. So, if TV is your medium of choice, before you make travel plans, check on the TV opportunities.

Another difficulty with TV is that guest interviews are short (typically 3 to 5 minutes), so you must really have good sound bites. Getting your "schtick" down and your message clear is of paramount importance for successful TV appearances.

Practice makes perfect. Video cameras are now easy to operate. Many phones now have video capabilities to record a mock TV appearance. How do you look? Do you appear comfortable? Friendly?

Defensive? Is your red shirt your best color? Does that tie match that shirt? Are your shoes clean and polished? Do your clothes fit well? Are they clean and pressed? Insignificant details? Hardly. How you look represents something very significant: a first impression.

If you enjoy looking down a camera lens while answering more of the same questions that were asked on previous shows, then TV is definitely right for you.

TV audiences are harsh judges. No, you need not lose 20 or 30 pounds if you're overweight, or even change your hairstyle if you're not happy with your appearance. But do stay aware of these kinds of details and change whatever you feel should be improved about your appearance.

Celebritize Yourself Fact:

"TV creates trends. It can also lend huge credibility to you, or your book, product, or service."

Print Is King!

I repeat! "Print is king!"

Why? Because anything written is perceived to be true. For instance, articles that quote you give you immediate positioning as an expert in your field. And the print media is **always** where a huge segment of your buying audience will come from.

Over 150 million Americans read daily newspapers. There are more than 31,000 publications – on topics ranging from antiques to zoology. So clearly print media holds mass appeal as a key source to entertain and inform.

Perhaps the most attractive aspect of print media is the huge variety of publications you can target – daily and weekly newspapers, local and national magazines, trade publications, news search engines, blogs, and Internet article banks. The publications to target are endless.

Another terrific aspect of this medium is the opportunity to edit. While this takes time, it adds the benefit of rehearsal. Radio and TV are both wonderful mediums if your mind thinks quickly and you can spew sound bites while under pressure on the air.

The printed media is a more cautious and careful media. Most interviews are via email where you can take a day or two – or at the very least, an hour or two if a deadline looms. This gives you a chance to self-edit your answers. You can more carefully consider and reconsider the best way to convey your message when answering the interviewer's question. This is media gold – a rare opportunity to better control your responses and give readers your perspective.

Speaking of time, when it comes to print you must understand newspaper and magazine timelines. Newspapers have tight deadlines, so if you have a hot news story or a great event planned, get your story to the paper immediately or it's no longer "news." Magazines have a much longer lead time. Monthly publications can schedule their issues 3 to 6 months ahead. So, make sure that you pitch your story far enough in advance to be one of the select few who will be selected.

Other celebrities, PR firms, corporate PR Executives, and marketers compete for coveted editorial coverage. So, do your research. You must know *who* to pitch, *when* to pitch, and most of all, *"how."* The "how" tips are most important:

- Build a compelling story;
- Develop a story angle that will interest the broadest spectrum of publications;

- Create a strong headline for your message;

- Keep your pitch newsworthy, entertaining, and informative;

- Whenever possible, provide good quality photographs to support your story.

Here's another very successful approach: write informative articles with your byline. Publications always want valuable information for their readers. Don't forget, as the radio host or TV anchor plays to their audience to earn high ratings, the print media plays to their readers to increase their publication's circulation.

A major endeavor? No doubt. But worth the effort a million times over when an interview takes place or your article runs with your photo alongside. And don't discount the importance of coverage in smaller publications. Every newspaper story, sidebar, small mention or feature story is gold. It might also grab the attention of editors at the national major magazines or the senior producers of national TV shows.

Celebritize Yourself Fact:

*"The print media is **always** where a huge segment of your buying audience will come from."*

Chapter 10:

Now Let's Get Started!

"Even if you are on the right track,
you will get run over if you just sit there."

~ Will Rogers

So, what is the official "game plan" to celebritize yourself? As I tell my clients, this chapter is where the "rubber meets the road." I assume that you now have the skills necessary to bring your message to market: passion, drive, perseverance, patience, and potential.

You're also confident that there is great need for people like yourself because the media *always* needs experts to comment on the news. Endless news cycles and the need for fresh, informed, upbeat faces drive celebrity – and credibility – in the news business. This is no less so for the multitude of cable news channels that keep viewers, readers, and listeners tuned in.

History is made by the people who simply show up. So is celebrity. Behind your TV screen, out of earshot on your radio, and just past the boldface print of your newspaper and Web pages hustles a busy industry of people who, quite literally, "make the news." This non-stop, 24-hour process requires massive amounts of material to keep moving. There is no shortage of opportunity for the would-be celebrity. But you must *show up* to stake your claim. You must also take the proper steps to get the biggest results.

The bridge between yourself and the infinite news media comes down to one thing and one thing only: **access.** You must successfully access the media gatekeepers, secretaries, assistants, assistant producers, and even *interns* to secretaries, assistants, and assistant producers.

You do not gain access with neon press kits or with bells and whistles added to your email messages. Nor can you badger these people with endless voicemail messages. No matter how clever YOU might consider these tactics to be, you can only gain access through credibility. You must create an identity for yourself that is synonymous with expertise in some specific area of need, whether it is fitness, management, cooking, inventions, leadership, self-help, or a do-it-yourself home repair.

They say that to write well you must "show, don't tell." The same is true with the media. They don't want promises, they want results. Don't tell them what you CAN do, show them what you have done. Give reasons, specific reasons, backed up by numbers and benefits – why YOU can help THEM. What do you offer their readers, listeners, or viewers? Be credible. Provide newsworthy information. Those are the twin keys to get past today's very skillful gatekeepers.

This credibility, these results – based on your knowledge, identity and message – are what we've built so far. It's what earlier chapters of this book were about. Now let's shift that focus, relay that message, and garner credibility to get you access to the media.

To celebritize yourself, the challenge is to find ways to make your message, brand, and identity known to local and national media. Become an "expert" they call on to educate and entertain their audiences. Their Rolodexes – electronic or otherwise – are precious. It's where they list their repository of prospective guests. Encourage them to highlight your name!

Ask yourself: will they recognize your name when they see it on a pink message slip or in their email inbox? What will make them call you before they call other prospective guests? What will you add to their program, article, or profile?

It's always a war of attrition. You speak and publish and print and offer and do signings and readings. You use your book as your entrée into this world of media. And you do it again and again and again.

The process is always a whisper – a repeated, collective whisper – never a shout. That is how they equate your name with your book. That's how it starts. "Oh yeah, that guy who wrote the book on home repair on a shoestring budget?" Or, "Oh, right, that gal who exercises underwater and lost 50 pounds?" It's okay if your message comes before your name; in fact it's better that your message comes before your name. Your message is important enough – valuable enough – to make **your name** memorable to the media decision-makers.

Eventually you will be more than a name. You are an author. Eventually, you are more than an author. You are an expert. "Oh yeah, that interesting guy with the do-it-yourself book I saw on that cable show last week? Let's see if he has any comment about that new gizmo I saw at Home Depot." Or, "Oh, right, that attractive girl with the underwater exercise program I heard on my drive home last night? Does she have any tips about how to stay in shape over the holidays?"

Never forget that you must offer value to the media. Until you are useful to producers, news anchors, talk show hosts, and journalists, it won't matter how good your book or your message is. The media must see you as an "audience getter" or **they won't return your calls.** You must quickly make them see how beneficial your personal, unique and fresh approach is to whatever you're writing or talking about before they'll return your calls.

For that objective, you need a solid game plan, one that will win this war of attrition. You must stay constantly aware of what's in the news and, more importantly, how to shape your message to timely events.

Constantly add to your network of secretaries, assistants, producers, editors, talk shows hosts and, yes, even intern gatekeepers. Know whom to contact when it's time to remind them of your expertise or your book or to once again give them your contact information.

But wait, I'm getting a bit ahead of myself.

Celebritize Yourself Fact:
*"The bridge between yourself and the infinite news media comes down to one thing and one thing only: **access.**"*

Pepper the News With Your Own Insights

Knowledge IS power. Read your newspapers. Watch TV news. Listen to AM talk radio. What issues or news stories tie in with your business or message? Keep clippings and Internet bookmarks updated with relevant stories from which to draw quotes, tidbits, and statistics.

Sound daunting? It's less so if you streamline your efforts. Find one or two Web sites that collect and continually update 24/7 news feeds on a wide variety of topics – world, domestic, health, business, science – to easily spot the top-5 headlines. Check often. (Yahoo! NEWS and CNN.com are great!)

Immediate access to the latest news is crucial to connect with the media, because the media follows the news and current news information is part of their programming.

It's not just today's news. It's tomorrow's as well. Stay ahead of trends. Predict what's just around the corner – whether it is a holiday, election, or significant anniversary of some national or local tragedy or celebration.

Don't force the connections, but do seek and find them. Not every news event will tie into your exercise program, cookbook, leadership seminar, or home repair manual, but they will more often than you might think they will. Still, the only way to use what's in the news is to track it voraciously.

Organize your links, clippings and bookmarks. Files get fat fast when you become a newshound, so separate the wheat from the chaff. Target the news items that will work for you.

For instance, if your topic is health or fitness, forget the sports daily. Start with the health and lifestyle section. Read about new diets and nutrition supplements. Many news sites categorize their hourly updates into entertainment, nutrition, health and so forth. Start there and work concentrically. If a famous celebrity is in yet another story or on yet another magazine cover looking shockingly heavy, wouldn't that be a great opener for local or national media about your weight-loss book?

Likewise, if your book is about business, leadership, or management, follow the news trends, stories and updates within *Fortune.com* or the *Wall Street Journal.* No need to track Yahoo's Entertainment section or *Sports Illustrated.*

Focus. Aim. Persistence. Three skills you need to stay abreast of the news that matters to you and your success!

Celebritize Yourself Fact:

"It's not just today's news. It's tomorrow's as well. Stay ahead of trends."

How to Pitch Yourself to the Media: Top 5 Tips

A pitch is not a pitch is not a pitch. Huh? What? This simply means that not all pitches are equal. What's more, the gatekeepers hear pitches all day long. Every day. And they hear some real doozies. Trust me. I know. That's my business.

That's the problem with pitches; so many people make them so badly that it puts every pitch – including yours – in a bad light. Guilt by association. Ask yourself, "What would perk my ears if I had to listen to bad pitches all day? How might I make my message stand out to someone who is brain-dead about still another pitch?"

The good new is that it's not hard to stand out against the run-of-the-mill media pitch. But just as you get savvier with every page of this book, so, too can your competition (if they're reading my book). To stay competitive you must constantly hone your pitch to get it right over the plate each and every time. So, here are my top 5 tips:

1. **Never pitch yourself.** Instead, pitch the ISSUE with which you are expert. The media hears from self-proclaimed "experts" all day long. But it's the topic, issue, or trend of your expertise that peaks the interest of the producer.

2. **Never pitch your product.** Pitch the PROBLEM your product solves. The media is all about results for their audiences who want information fast and want it to be right. They want answers, not questions; solutions, not problems. So, show

them that you are prepared with facts, statistics, research and your own knowledge and expertise to either answer a topical question or solve a current problem.

3. **Give them the story.** Although the media will do their own homework, they don't rely on their research alone. Give them YOUR facts. Give them the storyline. (That's why you have your file folder and Internet bookmarks!) Producers, editors, and their assistants are busy. They can't stay abreast of every last-second shift in statistics or latest research study. Your job is to let them know what's going on and to create a compelling story in which you can be the superstar.

4. **Make the right choices.** If you're pitching a controversial radio or TV show, recommend additional guests who might want to appear with you. This gives you more control of the segment and fortifies your message.

5. **Be flexible.** Not every pitch works every time, but a good pitch **will eventually work.** Be ready to speak on a multitude of issues that relate to your core message. Be prepared, be knowledgeable, and above all be flexible.

Celebritize Yourself Fact:

"The media is all about results for their audiences who want information fast and want it to be right. They want answers, not questions; solutions, not problems."

Appear on Talk Radio Shows Nationwide

You need broad exposure for several reasons. To start, it's a great way to build your credibility as a celebrity and gain national exposure. It's how you reach the masses. As importantly, talk radio has the most educated, affluent, and attentive audiences – individuals you want to speak to. Educated, affluent, and attentive audiences are most likely to buy.

Anyone can get their message heard. Stop traffic, go to rehab, rob a bank, get kicked off an island, stand naked in the middle of a football field. People will pay attention – for a few seconds. Perhaps a few minutes. But then what?

A great big noise – like a sudden round of applause – can boost your ego, but it doesn't always produce big sales. **You want lightning, not thunder.** An audience that is educated pays attention. They listen, ask probing questions and want to learn more. The affluent's quest for knowledge results in sales of your book, product, service or weekend seminar package. You name it. An audience that's attentive remembers your name, message, book title, Web site address or 800 number. They want to know more about you.

The audience that's all three – educated, affluent, and attentive – spreads the word with loyalty and lightning speed. Isn't that what you want?

Don't forget, radio interviews are easy to do from your home or office and there are thousands of shows who need and want expert guests such as yourself.

That's great news for you.

It's *greater* news for your celebrity.

Celebritize Yourself Fact:

"...talk radio has the most educated, affluent, and attentive audiences – individuals you want to speak to. Educated, affluent, and attentive audiences are most likely to buy."

7 Reasons Why Talk Radio Gives You Celebrity Status Faster

Believe in doing what works for you. I've counseled enough clients to know that you can't force them to stray too far from their comfort zones. Some clients will never feel comfortable talking before a camera. They might wow an audience – and many impress me one-on-one – but some mental block prevents them from shining on TV.

Why force it? Why spend too much time and energy nagging these folks to go on camera? Why not instead book them on radio or get stories about them in newspapers and magazines? Why reinvent the wheel when you can more easily roll down the highway at a pretty fast clip on radio?

So, if radio is within your comfort zone, or if it appeals to you more than TV or print, there's never been a better time for you to prosper on the airwaves. But don't take only my word for it. With 1,000 plus talk radio interviews under his belt, media personality Dr. William Wong can tell you, "Talk radio is the greatest way to get your message across to a large group of people at one time. There's a captive audience during morning and evening drive times, in the middle of the day with working people, and also late at night audiences. Without question, talk radio gives the best promotional bang for the buck!"

Talk radio is probably one of the best-kept marketing secrets! Here are seven reasons for starters:

1. **The Right Demographics:** Every year, *Talkers Magazine* (a leading radio industry trade publication) profiles the talk radio listener. Each year their survey confirms that the talk radio listener is, *"diverse, educated, attentive, active and affluent..."* If this describes the listener you want, you have a perfect match!

2. **Target Audiences.** Aside from the great demographics, you can easily reach your target audience. Specialty talk shows on finance, law, politics, health, relationships, lifestyles, consumer advocacy, sports, gardening and more allows you to identify shows that **perfectly match your message.**

3. **Effective Sales Tool.** Publicity can be **far more effective** than paid advertising. A compelling talk radio interview can sell your product or service without the audience realizing you're selling or that they've been sold! With a good interview, your listeners will want to know how to get whatever you are talking about. Most hosts will freely mention your Web site address or toll-free number so you – not they – get bombarded with phone calls, while accommodating their listening audience.

4. **Third-Party Endorsement.** Talk radio hosts have loyal audiences. That's how they keep their high ratings. Listeners tune in daily to hear their favorite host. That host is considered an old friend or trusted advisor, so when you appear as a guest on their show, listeners take that as **an implicit endorsement of you and your message!**

5. **Credibility.** This is a crucial ingredient in every marketing campaign! Talk radio supplies it in abundance. One client told

us, *"...on every show on which I've appeared, the host tells his listeners about my great expertise, my many accomplishments, and how proud he is to have me as a guest on his show! Of course, the more important I seem as a guest, the more important the host appears to be. For promotional credibility – it just doesn't get any better!"*

6. **Enough Time to Tell Your Whole Story.** As a guest, you have far more than 60 seconds of airtime - *you have ten to sixty minutes of quality time* with a targeted, attentive audience. You have time to effectively tell your story and talk about the quality of your products or services and how they can benefit the listeners. It's a perfect opportunity to promote yourself to the masses, and to generate those big sales!

7. **Cost Effective Promotion.** Most talk radio interviews are done by phone, no need to travel to the station. Think about it, you can have live conversations from your home or office, with potential new clients living anywhere around the country.

Celebritize Yourself Fact:

"A compelling talk radio interview can sell your product or service without the audience realizing that you're selling or that they've been sold!"

The Focus Is On You: 3 Proven Techniques To Get Talk Radio Hosts To Promote You And Your Book

Many successful authors and publishers agree that talk radio is the perfect media to promote almost any non-fiction title. Authors of how-to books, financial advice books, self-help books, travel books, medical books, even history books – nearly any non-fiction genre – all make attractive guests. This is because talk show hosts like to present their listeners with useful information from an expert. Fiction authors face more of an uphill battle to land talk radio interviews, or to get any major media exposure for that matter. No, it's not impossible, but it's not easy, either.

Your challenge as a non-fiction author is to get hosts and producers interested in you and your topic, then to interest them in having you as a guest on their show. Fortunately, for nearly two decades, my firm has developed a number of innovative tried-and-true techniques to promote both the nonfiction and fiction author. These techniques I can now reveal to you.

Technique # 1:
Tout Your Strongest Selling Point

The first thing we look at when creating a talk radio pitch is the author's profession, background, hobbies, or experience. What is fascinating, glamorous or downright interesting about the author? How can we present these strengths in a way that will get a host to want more information?

One of our clients, a former judge on the Arizona Supreme Court, wrote a great book about what goes on in the judicial system. We knew the angle "had just so many legs." We played it for as long as we could to keep the media's interest, but knew that eventually we had to find some new angles.

Our job requires us to have a good pulse on what the public is currently thinking about. We knew that his profession alone would make him a compelling guest. By positioning him as a judge who could also comment on legal issues in the news (and there are plenty of those), we generated a great deal of interest in having him as a guest for spot appearances. Consequently, he appeared on more than a hundred shows throughout the country. Each interview was another opportunity to discuss and plug his book.

Technique # 2:
Mine Your Message

After we've scoped out our author's background, we next look at the author's key message and how it might tie into current events or hot news. One instance was the client who wrote a book instructing people on how to plan their "estates." The Terri Schiavo controversy was raging at that time. Naturally, we tied our author's book into the ongoing national debate. You can see how this author became a hot commodity on talk radio, gaining huge media attention for himself and his book.

If somehow we can't focus the pitch around the author or a current event, then we try to find something about the book that people can relate to. This is our "secret" for promoting fiction authors. A good example was an author who came aboard with an interesting fiction title, but the story didn't tie into current news. Nor was our author a known name. Still, we found a storyline most people could relate to that our author could expertly talk about. "Does sibling rivalry ever end?" This subject struck a chord with so many hosts and producers, that our client landed more interviews than she could possibly handle. Yes, there's an interesting twist to talk about in any book.

Technique # 3:
Be Yourself

We are experts in talk radio placement so we are often asked how we can book 50 to 100 interviews a week while staying within our own strict qualifications of cities and stations we work with. The answer is simple: yes, we have close relationships with many hosts and producers. But even more fundamental is that we know what the media wants in a guest and, that's what we give them. That's why the media constantly calls us to book their next great guest.

And now you know what they're looking for, too!

Celebritize Yourself Fact:

"Your challenge as a non-fiction author is to get hosts and producers interested in you and your topic – then interest them in having you as a guest on their show."

"Tips" Articles Can Create Big Buzz

One easy, inexpensive way to get free publicity in newspapers, magazines, trade publications and e-mags is to offer valuable advice. Make sure to include your credentials and other self-serving information to position yourself as the expert who wrote the article.

This should be a piece of cake for you. Big author of a book and all? Seriously though, tips articles can greatly help build your credentials and enhance your message. Are you a nutrition expert? Think of something new and unique to say about America's struggle with obesity or the new trend in "energy drinks." Does your book deal with leadership? Condense one chapter into an article for a newspaper, magazine, or Web site.

Don't stop there; publish, publish, and publish some more. Did you read a good book while researching your topic? Review it and post the review on Amazon.com. Include your name and author credit. Write stories for your local paper, answer calls for submissions on your favorite Web sites, blogs, or journals, and always use your book's name and your credentials in your byline.

The world is shrinking. Every blog, magazine, TV show, or radio program brings us closer, not farther apart. Share your message often and widely. The nice thing about the written word is its permanence. Once on a Web site, it usually stays for a long time. It stays in the archive, on links, or in recent articles. Someone will read it!

Posting comments to someone else's blog is the same as placing your article there. Your name is there. That is added value. Not writing prolifically for today's new media is no different than never leaving your couch while complaining that the bus never stops to pick you up.

For the driver to see you, you must get up and wave him down.

For the world to know you , you must introduce yourself.

Celebritize Yourself Fact:

"Publish, publish, and publish some more."

Send Letters to the Opinion Editor

Become a letter writer. Articles, comments, and book reviews are all formal styles of writing that can take weeks or even months to master. But we all grew up writing letters, right?

Rekindle the joy of jotting down your thoughts for someone special by writing letters. And write a lot of them. Send a letter to the Op-Ed section of your local paper with your opinion or editorial position. It's not exactly news, but your comment on the news may get published, giving you exposure.

Good arguments can well express or promote your point of view. Remember, the more exposure you get, the more credibility you gain, particularly with the local press. Your goal: become their "go to" person for your particular topic.

But for them to "go to" you they must know you're out there!

Celebritize Yourself Fact:
"Rekindle the joy of jotting down your thoughts for someone special by writing letters. And write a lot of them."

Photo Opportunities Abound!

Words are great. But how many words is a single picture worth? Many wordy types shy away from the camera, but what celebrity do you know who is camera shy?

None. Because celebrities know the value of a good photo.

Local newspapers and TV want interesting photos and images. But how do you get your photos in the media? Invite them to your events. The media may not show up, which is why you should invest in a digital camera. Snap a few dozen photos at the event, download your photos, then forward them with a press release to the media.

Don't wait for great photo ops. Create them. Think beyond the camera lens. If you've already taken the same "local author does book signing" photos a dozen times, step back and rethink. How can you make the signing (and thus the photos) more interesting?

Be creative to stand out from the crowd. One author regularly scheduled her book signings, appearances, and readings at local venues around the holidays. She always dressed accordingly – patriotically for Independence Day or Memorial Day, all green for St. Patrick's Day, and so forth. She also themed the event accordingly.

On St. Patrick's Day, "green beers" turned into "green bookmarks" featuring her book. They were a big hit with the crowd and, naturally, made for great digital photos for the local media. Few turned her down.

A quick personal postscript here. Several years ago my non-profit, Cherish the Children Foundation, received a $10,000 donation for us to host a "Back to School" event for our community's disadvantaged children. We purchased all types of school supplies; rulers, erasers, pads, pens, pencils, glue, and dictionaries, all to be carried in beautiful new backpacks.

Donors always want to know that their money is well spent. What better demonstration of this than press coverage of the event? Of course, we invited the press, but we also had our own photographer and pre-written press releases ready had they not shown up.

Our "Back to School" event was a great human interest story and our local major daily newspaper ran a great photo of the children with beaming smiles as our volunteers filled their backpacks with goodies! The best part was the quote that ran with the photo about our charity, with glowing recognition of the organization that funded our event. This photo op was a perfect "thank you" to our donor.

You see, the point is as long as your event matches your message, great photos can give you priceless press coverage.

Celebritize Yourself Fact:
"Don't wait for great photo ops. Create them."

Buzz, Buzz, Buzz, and More Buzz

Get onto the speaking circuit in your community and within your industry. Speak to community groups, at Chambers of Commerce events, and to trade associations. Create buzz about yourself and your company.

And, always invite the media!

Creating buzz is like anything else, it takes time. Buzz is just like a Web site; unless you tell people about it, no one will find it.

Buzz building is also like credibility building; you must prove yourself time and again. Keep your appearances fresh, updated, light and appealing. Be different from the comedian who tells the same jokes in 200 different towns across all 50 states. Whether you speak to 5 people at a round-table discussion, 50 people at a charity luncheon, or 500 people at a leadership conference, always be yourself and personalize your message to the audience.

Update your statistics, research, and message. Dress professionally and be alert. Never mistake "just another speaking gig" for just another speaking gig. Every public appearance is one more opportunity for you to impress and for people to judge you. While you should feel comfortable and relaxed – it's not the State of the Union address, after all – you should likewise feel passionate and purposeful about your appearance.

Should the media appear, they'll recognize an alert, intelligent, capable expert as opposed to just another wannabe making the rounds of the local press circuit. They will court the former and ignore the latter. But even if the media isn't there, treat every audience with respect and reverence. Remember, the audience is the cake, the media the icing.

Celebritize Yourself Fact:

"Buzz is just like a Web site; unless you tell people about it, no one will find it."

Saving the Hottest Tip for Last:
How to Become a Celebrity Talk Show Host

Here's a little-known secret: a large number of radio shows heard on the weekends are paid programming. That means those hosts buy the air time or find sponsors to pay for the time. Buying air time is an amazingly affordable marketing tool and one of the most effective ways to celebritize yourself.

Imagine your own weekly show, "Ask the Legal Expert" or the "Health Expert" or the "Real Estate," "Martial Arts," "Fitness," "Diet," "Finance Expert," and so forth. Nevertheless, when people are driving or listening from home, they hear <u>your</u> show on the air. You're an immediate celebrity in the public's eye. The public immediately identifies you as an expert.

Here's a wonderful example. I once caught a chiropractor's radio show when traveling across the state. He was indeed a master. Listeners would call in with questions about their health and he had the knack of sounding as if he and the caller were together in a private room in his clinic. His helpful advice was delivered with the most compassionate, caring bedside manner.

The airwaves made him the ideal doctor – one who everyone wants at their bedside when they don't feel well. He would, of course, invite each caller to come to his office to continue the conversation. Each caller felt that it was a special invitation from this caring, thoughtful doctor. His ability to fill the airwaves with his compassionate tone was a most amazing skill. His office had to be flooded with new patients week after week from his own paid show.

But, why stop locally? If your goal is to be a national celebrity, then you can build your show market by market. Gradually you can become a national personality. It's done all the time.

And why stop with radio? If you have the charm, looks, engaging personality, and a message that will appeal to the masses – go TV. You have similar opportunities to create your own TV show, whether locally or nationally.

Celebritize Yourself Fact:

"Buying air time is an amazingly affordable marketing tool and one of the most effective ways to celebritize yourself."

Chapter 11:
The Big Payoff

"Success is not the key to happiness. Happiness is the key to success. If you love what you are doing, you will be successful."

~ Albert Schweitzer

L et me take this one final opportunity to get you excited about *Celebritizing Yourself.* I hope that I've succeeded, because if you're not energized to become a celebrity by now then you might never be.

But you are – admit it!

If you dare to look into that crystal ball, then you can almost see, touch, and feel the rewards to be had. It's exciting to think about doing something you love, sharing your knowledge and expertise, touching people's lives, making new friends, seeing new places, and learning new things about yourself and others. This is what the journey is all about. And, let's not forget the potential for huge financial success. That all comes with the territory.

Okay – you're with me. I'm so glad! Now all that remains is to get started. That's your next step. Apply the very principles we've explored to your own, personal passion and expertise. Whether it's helping others stay fit and healthy, teaching leadership and management skills, new ways to budget your money, or do-it-yourself home repair, what you have to say is special and unique. And, be assured, there IS always an interest in new ideas and new viewpoints. That's the beauty of our society.

Remind yourself that celebrity is not a means to an end. It's an ongoing journey. It is a path, not a destination. To walk that path takes a strong commitment to develop your message, write your book, captivate your audience, and build your credibility. Mostly, it takes a strong commitment to YOURSELF, and to YOUR OWN SUCCESS and HAPPINESS.

Many want to start this journey, but never do. Many start, but never finish. Let me share what the famous aviator Amelia Earhart wrote, "The most difficult thing is the decision to act, the rest is merely tenacity. The fears are paper tigers. You can do anything you decide to do. You can act to change and control your life; and the procedure, the process is its own reward." I couldn't agree with Amelia more.

Don't let the hard work disillusion you or the obstacles stand in your way. If you keep the faith, and apply the principles in this book (and other principles that you learn along the way), you *will* find the journey getting easier, the applause growing louder, and the reward turning out to be everything you hoped for.

Getting to know yourself intimately – a requisite for any celebrity – can often become the birth (or rebirth) of a brand new you. I am eager to hear about your successes, your challenges, your good times, and your bad. There will be potholes in the road to celebrity as well as mountains you thought you could never climb.

I want to hear about your entire journey. Contact me at www.marshafriedman.com.. Share with me your personal stories, your aspirations and let's see how we can help you achieve celebrity. Your success is my reward!

Celebritize Yourself Fact:

"Celebrity is not a means to an end. It's an ongoing journey. It is a path, not a destination."

About the Author:
Marsha Friedman

Marsha Friedman is a prominent businesswoman, publicity expert, radio personality, and public speaker. Her company, EMSI (Event Management Services, Inc), is a national public relations firm. Launched in 1990, her firm represents corporations and experts in a wide array of fields such as business, health and fitness, food and beverage, travel and lifestyle, politics, technology, finance, law, sports, and entertainment. Some of the more prominent names on her client roster are Teamster's President Jimmy Hoffa Jr., Sergeant's Pet Care Products, former National Security advisor Robert McFarlane, and the famous Motown group, the Temptations.

She consults individuals and businesses on a daily basis and is frequently asked to speak at conferences about how to harness the power of publicity.

Outside of the office, Marsha can be heard every week with her co-hosts on the nationally syndicated talk radio show "The Family Roundtable" (www.myfamilyroundtable.com) where they discuss problems that modern families face. Marsha and her co-hosts have enjoyed interviewing family experts as well as celebrities such as Ed Begley Jr., Augusten Burroughs, Denise Jackson, Janine Turner, Rose Rock, and Vicki Lawrence.

Additionally, Marsha enjoys giving back to the community that has served her. A mother of three and a grandmother who raised one of her grandchildren, she is the founder of the non-profit organization, Cherish the Children Foundation. In 1996 the White House recognized her charity which sets out to raise awareness of the plight of underprivileged and foster children.

Bibliography

Boldt, G. Lawrence. *Zen and the Art of Making a Living: A Practical Guide to Creative Career Design.* New York: Penguin. 1999.

Canfield, Jack, and Mark Victor Hansen. *The Aladdin Factor: How to Ask For and Get Everything You Want.* New York: Berkley Trade. 1995.

Chang, Larry, and Roderick Terry. *Wisdom for the Soul of Black Folk.* New York: Gnosophia Publishers. 2007.

Chang, Larry. *Wisdom for the Soul: Five Millennia of Prescriptions for Spiritual Healing.* New York: Gnosophia Publishers. 1995.

Hume, Ellen. "Resource Journalism: A Model for New Media." *Democracy and New Media.* Eds. Jenkins, Henry, and David Thorbum. Cambridge: The MIT Press. 2004.

Lederer, Richard. *The Miracle of Language.* New York: Pocket. 1999.

Pincott, J. *Success: Advice for Achieving Your Goals from Remarkably Accomplished People.* New York: Random House, Inc. 2005.

Safire, William, and Leonard Safire. *Words of Wisdom: More Good Advice.* New York: Simon and Schuster. 1989.

Uhles, Steven. **"Rascal Flatts is more than country, singer says."** *The Augusta Chronicle.* May 17, 2002.

Ziglar, Zig. *Secrets of Closing the Sale.* New York: Berkley Trade. 1985.